COLLECTED POEMS

EDWIN MUIR
A photograph taken in 1955 when he was 68

EDWIN MUIR, 1887 — 1959.

*

Collected Poems

New York
OXFORD UNIVERSITY PRESS
1965

To Willa

PREFACE

As my correspondence files indicate, it was only in the last years of Edwin Muir's life, when he brought his later poems to me for publication, that I saw much of him, and I cannot say that I ever came to know him really intimately. He was a reserved, reticent man, not fluent in conversation. Yet his personality made a deep inpression upon me, and especially the impression of one very rare and precious quality. There have been other encounters in my life with men who have left me with the impression of this particular quality, including several men whom I have never come to know well. They have been those men of whom I should say without hesitation, that they were men of complete *integrity*. And as I have grown older, I have come to realise how rare this quality is. That utter honesty with oneself and with the world is no more common among men of letters than among men of other occupations. I stress this unmistakeable integrity, because I came to recognise it in Edwin Muir's work as well as in the man himself. The work and the man are one: his autobiography, and the lecture on Orcadian folk poetry, which is the first of his Norton lectures at Harvard, help us to understand his own poetry. And I cannot believe that Edwin Muir ever uttered one disingenuous word in speech, or committed one disingenuous word to print.

I do not remember when, or in what context, we first met. I seem to remember him, in earlier days, as a contributor to the *New English Weekly*. It would have been characteristic of Orage, in whose papers so many notable writers made their appearance, to discover this shy man of genius. But I must admit that in my youth I gave very little heed to Muir's poetry. His poetry was not of the kind which I was trying to write myself, and it was not until after my own lines of development were well established that it began to appeal to me. How much of this late appeal was due to the maturing of Muir's power, and how much to the maturing of my own taste, I cannot tell. A young poet is apt to be indifferent to the work of a contemporary who is following a different path from his own. But when I came to study the volume of his *Collected Poems*, before publication, I was struck, as I had not been before, by the power of his early work. Yet on the other hand it is still his late work which seems to me the most remarkable.

In my earlier years, or rather in the second phase of my development, I went through a period of concentrating my attention on experiment in metric and language. It may be that to focus my conscious mind in this way helped to release my imagination. For some poets, perhaps, this experiment with forms of verse and with varieties of expression may remain a permanent preoccupation. I do not believe that technique was ever a primary concern with Edwin. He was first and foremost deeply concerned with what he had to say—and by that I do not mean that his purpose was ever didactic or that he was striving to convey a "message." But under the pressure of emotional intensity, and possessed by his vision, he found, almost unconsciously, the right, the inevitable way of saying what he wanted to say.

Kathleen Raine wrote a review of Edwin Muir's *Collected Poems* in *The New Statesman* for April 23, 1960, which I hope she will reprint in some volume of essays, and which I can say little to supplement. But I should like to add this one thought. Edwin Muir will remain among the poets who have added glory to the English language. He is also one of the poets of whom Scotland should always be proud. But there is, furthermore, it seems to me, something essential which is neither English nor Scottish, but Orcadian. There is the sensibility of the remote islander, the boy from a simple primitive offshore community who then was plunged into the sordid horror of industrialism in Glasgow, who struggled to understand the modern world of the metropolis in London and finally the realities of central Europe in Prague where he and his wife— to whom together we owe our knowledge of Kafka—saw the iron curtain fall and where they saw their friends gradually finding it safer to avoid their company. And all of this experience is somehow concentrated into that great, that terrifying poem of the "atomic age"—*The Horses*.

T.S. ELIOT

AUTHOR'S NOTE

I wish to thank J. C. Hall first of all for the generous care and discrimination which made possible, at a time when I had little opportunity to deal with it, the publication of the predecessor to this volume, *Collected Poems 1921–1951*. My thanks are due next to The Hogarth Press for allowing me to reprint nine poems from *First Poems*, and to Messrs. J. M. Dent and Sons, Ltd., for permission to include the full text of *Variations on a Time Theme* and most of the poems in *Journeys and Places*. All the poems selected by Mr. Hall remain in the present edition, but I have added twenty-seven more from the earlier volumes, chosen because they express certain things which I wished to say at the time and have not said in the same way again. But for Mr. Hall's extreme kindness in the first place, it would have been difficult to do this now. The present volume contains also most of the poems in *One Foot in Eden*, which were written after the publication of the first collected edition.

I have made one or two minor alterations to the earlier poems, but no major ones.   E.M.

NOTE ON THE FINAL SECTION

Edwin Muir died at Cambridge (England) on the third of January 1959, at the age of seventy-one, a few weeks after the foregoing introduction was written. It was then decided to include in this collection, as a final section, all the poems which had not previously appeared in book form. We are reasonably certain that all these belong to the last five years of Edwin Muir's life, and the majority to the last three. Within these limits, however, any attempt to arrange them chronologically would be largely guesswork. We therefore thought it more useful to group them according to their relative stages of completion.

Thus, the first twenty-two poems are known to have been published (although sometimes in slightly different versions) during Edwin Muir's lifetime, or to have been given by him to his publishers in typescript. These can be regarded as carrying the author's *imprimatur*. The next six poems were discovered among Edwin Muir's papers in typescript, but had not previously been published as far as is known. Some of these would no doubt have undergone further revision; it is obvious, for instance, that "Ballad of Everyman" and "Nightmare of Peace" are essentially versions of one poem. Finally, there is a group of poems or parts of poems which were found only in manuscript and needed deciphering. The first two are obviously incomplete, but it is more difficult to decide how complete some of the others are.

The last two poems in this book are almost certainly the last things that Edwin Muir wrote. They seem most fittingly to bring his work, as his life, to its close.

Willa Muir

J. C. Hall

NOTE ON THE SECOND EDITION

For the second edition we have made a few amendments in two poems in the final section, "Dialogue" ("I have heard you cry") and "I have been taught", and some minor typographical changes elsewhere. A hitherto uncollected poem, "The Two Sisters", first published in 1956, has been added to the final section. We are indebted to Professors Peter Butter and Robert Hollander for suggesting some of these changes after a close study of the texts.

W.M., J.C.H.

CONTENTS

FIRST POEMS (1925)

JOURNEYS AND PLACES (1937)

THE NARROW PLACE (1943)

THE VOYAGE (1946)

THE LABYRINTH (1949)

ONE FOOT IN EDEN (1956)

Part I

POEMS NOT PREVIOUSLY COLLECTED

I

First Poems

1925

CHILDHOOD

Long time he lay upon the sunny hill,
  To his father's house below securely bound.
Far off the silent, changing sound was still,
  With the black islands lying thick around.

He saw each separate height, each vaguer hue,
  Where the massed islands rolled in mist away,
And though all ran together in his view
  He knew that unseen straits between them lay.

Often he wondered what new shores were there.
  In thought he saw the still light on the sand,
The shallow water clear in tranquil air,
  And walked through it in joy from strand to strand.

Over the sound a ship so slow would pass
  That in the black hill's gloom it seemed to lie.
The evening sound was smooth like sunken glass,
  And time seemed finished ere the ship passed by.

Grey tiny rocks slept round him where he lay,
  Moveless as they, more still as evening came,
The grasses threw straight shadows far away,
  And from the house his mother called his name.

HORSES

Those lumbering horses in the steady plough,
On the bare field—I wonder why, just now,
They seemed terrible, so wild and strange,
Like magic power on the stony grange.

Perhaps some childish hour has come again,
When I watched fearful, through the blackening rain,
Their hooves like pistons in an ancient mill
Move up and down, yet seem as standing still.

Their conquering hooves which trod the stubble down
Were ritual that turned the field to brown,
And their great hulks were seraphim of gold,
Or mute ecstatic monsters on the mould.

And oh the rapture, when, one furrow done,
They marched broad-breasted to the sinking sun!
The light flowed off their bossy sides in flakes;
The furrows rolled behind like struggling snakes.

But when at dusk with steaming nostrils home
They came, they seemed gigantic in the gloam,
And warm and glowing with mysterious fire
That lit their smouldering bodies in the mire.

Their eyes as brilliant and as wide as night
Gleamed with a cruel apocalyptic light.
Their manes the leaping ire of the wind
Lifted with rage invisible and blind.

Ah, now it fades! it fades! and I must pine
Again for that dread country crystalline,
Where the blank field and the still-standing tree
Were bright and fearful presences to me.

BETRAYAL

Sometimes I see, caught in a snare,
    One with a foolish lovely face,
Who stands with scattered moon-struck air
    Alone, in a wild woody place.

She was entrapped there long ago.
    Yet fowler none has come to see
His prize; though all the tree-trunks show
    A front of silent treachery.

And there she waits, while in her flesh
    Small joyless teeth fret without rest.
But she stands smiling in the mesh,
    While she is duped and dispossest.

I know her name; for it is told
    That beauty is a prisoner,
And that her gaoler, bleak and bold,
    Scores her fine flesh, and murders her.

He slays her with invisible hands,
    And inly wastes her flesh away,
And strangles her with stealthy bands;
    Melts her as snow day after day.

Within his thicket life decays
    And slow is changed by hidden guile;
And nothing now of Beauty stays,
    Save her divine and witless smile.

For still she smiles, and does not know
    Her feet are in the snaring lime.
He who entrapped her long ago,
    And kills her, is unpitying Time.

WHEN THE TREES GROW BARE ON THE HIGH HILLS

When the trees grow bare on the high hills,
And through still glistening days
The wrinkled sun-memoried leaves fall down
From black tall branches
Through the gleaming air,
And wonder is lost,
Dissolving in space,
My heart grows light like the bare branches,
And thoughts which through long months
Have lain like lead upon my breast,
Heavy, slow-ripening thoughts,
Grow light and sere,
And fall at last, so empty and so beautiful.

And I become
Mere memory, mere fume
Of my own strife, my loud wave-crested clamour,
An echo caught
From the mid-sea
On a still mountain-side.
The leaves fall faster,
Like a slow unreturning fountain of red gold.
The billow of summer breaks at last
In far-heard whispering.
And in mere memory, mere dream,
Attainment breathes itself out,
Perfect and cold.

AUTUMN IN PRAGUE

The ripe fruit rests here,
On the chill ground,
In the sterile air,
All meanings have fallen into your lap,
Uncomprehending earth.

The stubble shines in the dry field,
Gilded by the pale sun.
The trees, unburdened, with light limbs,
Shiver in the cold light.
In the meadow the goat-herd,
A young girl,
Sits with bent head,
Blind, covered head,
Bowed to the earth,
Like a tree
Dreaming a long-held dream.

The gossamers forge their cables
Between the grasses,
Secure,
So still the blue air hangs its sea,
That great sea, so still!
The earth like a god,
Far withdrawn,
Lies asleep.

OCTOBER AT HELLBRUNN

The near-drawn stone-smooth sky, closed in and grey,
  Broods on the garden, and the turf is still.
The dim lake shines, oppressed the fountains play,
  And shadowless weight lies on the wooded hill.

The patient trees rise separate, as if deep
    They listened dreaming through the hollow ground,
Each in a single and divided sleep,
    While few sad leaves fall heedless with no sound.

The marble cherubs in the wavering lake
    Stand up more still, as if they kept all there,
The trees, the plots, in thrall. Their shadows make
    The water clear and hollow as the air.

The silent afternoon draws in, and dark
    The trees rise now, grown heavier is the ground,
And breaking through the silence of the park
    Farther a hidden fountain flings its sound.

BALLAD OF HECTOR IN HADES

Yes, this is where I stood that day,
    Beside this sunny mound.
The walls of Troy are far away,
    And outward comes no sound.

I wait. On all the empty plain
    A burnished stillness lies,
Save for the chariot's tinkling hum,
    And a few distant cries.

His helmet glitters near. The world
    Slowly turns around,
With some new sleight compels my feet
    From the fighting ground.

24

I run. If I turned back again
　　The earth must turn with me,
The mountains planted on the plain,
　　The sky clamped to the sea.

The grasses puff a little dust
　　Where my footsteps fall.
I cast a shadow as I pass
　　The little wayside wall.

The strip of grass on either hand
　　Sparkles in the light;
I only see that little space
　　To the left and to the right,

And in that space our shadows run,
　　His shadow there and mine,
The little flowers, the tiny mounds,
　　The grasses frail and fine.

But narrower still and narrower!
　　My course is shrunk and small,
Yet vast as in a deadly dream,
　　And faint the Trojan wall.
The sun up in the towering sky
　　Turns like a spinning ball.

The sky with all its clustered eyes
　　Grows still with watching me,
The flowers, the mounds, the flaunting weeds
　　Wheel slowly round to see.

Two shadows racing on the grass,
　　Silent and so near,
Until his shadow falls on mine.
　　And I am rid of fear.

25

The race is ended. Far away
  I hang and do not care,
While round bright Troy Achilles whirls
  A corpse with streaming hair.

BALLAD OF THE SOUL

I

I did not know whence came my breath
  Nor where had hid my clay,
Until my soul stood by my side
  As on my bed I lay.

I looked across a dark blue shore
  Under a dark blue sky,
The light came from no wandering star,
  The sun had not passed by.

Faintly uprose like graven mist
  A wraith upon the sea—
Woman or wraith or mist—I thought
  It made a sign to me.

The waters rose, down sank the land,
  The sea closed in like lead,
The waves like leopards tumbled on
  Far above my head.

There closed the mesh and waxed the flesh
  That brought my soul to birth.
I rose, the sky was white as snow,
  As ashes black the earth.

The ashes of memorial fires
    Extinguished utterly;
In towering blocks the twisted rocks
    Stuck up above the sea.

And now I swam, a moving thing
    On the vast and moveless mere,
And headless things swam all around;
    I saw and did not fear

Till when I reached the saving shore
    A soft sea-creature caught
My bonéd hand with boneless hand;
    For all a day I fought.

And it was gone. I walked alone
    Over sands and barren dunes;
The low-browed voiceless animals
    Were my companions.

II

What next I saw I cannot tell
    And ill can understand,
Though well I know that once I went
    Through that hollow land.

It was a waste of jagged rock
    (No beast nor bird was by),
And there what seemed a palace lay
    Like ruins of the sky.

I stood without, I stood within;
    Far down the toppling ledge,
Scaffolds of wood, scaffolds of wood
    From edge to yawning edge.

And spiders wove and silence lay
   On each deserted wall;
I poured myself from beam to beam,
   Dived deep and knew my fall,

And that one beam would hold me there
   And then like spouted light
That I should climb from beam to beam
   Until I scaled the height.

But now the roof with final seal
   Lay full upon my head;
My body like a battering ram
   Beat on it, beat and bled,
The blood dyed me head to foot
   Like a fierce fury red.

And the dumb stone shuddered and cried,
   Turned back and made a way.
The sky leapt up, the stars showered out,
   In peace the planets lay.

III

Now day came on me and I saw
   A tarn, a little mound,
And rushes like an army's spears
   Stood as at watch around.

Then on the white field of the sky
   Two clouds like phantoms fell.
They grew, they moved together like
   Two armies terrible.

They met, they broke in fiery smoke,
   A red ball in the sky,
A ball of fire, it raged and turned
   To ashes suddenly.

In the white sky a round black sun
   In furious circles whirled,
From which two serpents broke and shook
   Their flames over the world.

Their pennon fires shot out and in
   And split the cracking mail;
You'd say all hell with plumes of fire
   Upon the air did sail.

That sun drank up its fires, it stood
   In heaven immovably;
As if some fear had clamped it there
   It stood immovably.

But now its rage in furious spawn
   A hundred legs gave birth;
Like a great spider down the air
   It clambered to the earth.

Its head was like a wooden prow
   That had voyaged silently
Over the seas of perished worlds:
   It smiled disdainfully.

I stood; a sword was in my hand
   Fallen from the empty sky.
I struck the beast full on the brow,
   It did not move nor cry,

But like an image melting slow
   It softly, softly smiled.
My body was a storm wherethrough
   The sword in lightnings wild
Rove and rent: *it* sidewards bent
   Obedient as a child.

The sword streamed out in running fire,
   The hard mail burst in two,
The white-robed white-winged spirit up
   In wavering circles flew.

Hastily sank the empty mail
   Deep in the secret ground.
Nothing was there but trampled grass,
   The tarn, the watching mound.

IV

Then as l looked above I saw
   The sweet sky rain with wings.
I was so happy I longed to be
   With one of these fair things.

And now they flew over seas so clear
   That their bright wraiths below
Like mute and pilgrimaging thoughts
   Obediently did go.

Two linked their hands till one they seemed,
   Rose up in wavering rings;
Two plumes fell down the glittering air,
   They mounted on two wings.

I thought: Must these in mire be dipt,
   Reborn, take wings and fly,
And in such strange indifferent seas
   Their purity purify?

I asked, but then the fading dream
   Had nothing more to say
That night my soul stood by my side
   As on my bed I lay.

BALLAD OF THE FLOOD

"Last night I dreamed a ghastly dream,
   Before the dirl o' day.
A twining worm cam out the wast,
   Its back was like the slae.

"It ganted wide as deid men gant,
   Turned three times on its tail,
And wrapped itsel the warld around
   Till ilka rock did wail.

"Its belly was blacker than the coal,
   It wapped sae close about,
That it brak the hills in pieces sma'
   And shut the heavens out.

"Repent, repent, my folk, repent,
   Repent and turn around.
The hills are sinking in the sea,
   The warld has got a stound."

The braw lads woke beside their makes
  And drowsy were their een:
"O I wat this is anither day
  As every day has been.

"And we sall joy to-day, my luve,
  Sall dance to harp and horn,
And I'll devise anither play
  When we walk out the morn.

"But on the neist high day we twa
  Through the kirk door maun gae,
For sair I fear lest we sall brenn
  In living fire alway."

They looked around on every wa'
  And drowsy were their een.
The day rase up aboon the east
  As every day had been.

But Noah took a plank o' aik,
  Anither o' the pine,
And bigged a house for a' his folk
  To sail upon the brine.

"Gang out, gang out and ca' the beasts,
  Ca' twa o' every kind
To sail upon this crackling shell
  When a' the hills are blind.

"Ca' but, ca' but, and they'll rin fast
  As sune's they hear your voice,
For they hae heard amang the hills,
  I wat, a boding noise.

"They cry a' night about the house,
     And I hae ruth to see
Sae mony innocent creatures die
     For man's iniquity."

Noah's sons went out into the fields,
     Ca'd twa o' every kind.
They cam frae the east, they cam frae the wast,
     And followed close behind.

And some were brighter than the sun,
     Some blacker than the coal.
The lark was wiléd frae the sky,
     The serpent frae the hole.

And they were as meek as blessed sauls
     Assoilzied o' their sin,
They bowed their heids in thankfulness
     Whenas they entered in.

"Come in, come in, my people a',
     The sea has drunk the plain,
The hills are falling in the flood,
     The sun has downward gane."

The rain it rained baith day and night
     And the wind cam together.
The water rase in a lang straight line
     Frae ae hill to the tither.

The Ark span like a cockle shell,
     Ran east and then ran wast.
"Now God us save," auld Noah cried,
     "The warld is sinking fast."

The beasts they hid amang the shaws
   And loud and sair cried they.
They sabbed and maned the leelang night
   And fought the leelang day,

That the creatures in the Ark were sair
   Astonied at the sound.
They trembled sae they shak the house
   As it were in a swound.

But syne there was nae crying mair
   Across the dowie sea.
"I wat," said Noah, "the warld is sunk
   Frae plain to hill-top heigh."

The first day that auld Noah sailed
   The green trees floated by.
The second day that auld Noah sailed
   He heard a woman's cry.

And tables set wi' meats were there,
   Gowd beakers set wi' wine,
And twa lovers in a silken barge
   A-sailing on the brine.

They soomed upon the lanely sea
   And sad, sad were their een.
"O tak me in thy ship, auld man,
   And I'll please thee, I ween."

"Haud off, haud off," auld Noah cried,
   "Ye comena in to me!
Drown deep, drown deep, ye harlot fause,
   Ye wadna list to me."

She wrang her hands, she kissed her make,
    She lap into the sea.
But Noah turned and laughed fu' loud:
    "To hell, I wat, gang ye!

"To hell the haill warld gangs this day,
    But and my folk sae gude.
Sail on, sail on till Ararat
    Lifts up aboon the flood."

The third day that auld Noah sailed
    There was nae sign ava'.
The water rase on every side
    Like a weel biggéd wa'.

The astonied ships upon the sea
    Tacked round and round about
Till the dragons rising frae the deep
    Sucked a' their timbers out.

Ane after ane, ane after ane,
    They sank into the sea,
And there was nane left on the earth
    But the Ark's companie.

But every day the dragons came
    And played the Ark around.
They lay upon the faem and sang;
    It was a luvely sound.

"Why stand ye at the window, my sons?
    What hope ye there to see?"
"We wad see a gudely ha', faither,
    Set in the green countrie.

"But we see naught but water, water,
   We've seen this mony a day,
And the silly fishes in the faem
   That soom around in play."

"Sail on, sail on," auld Noah cried,
   "Sail on, sail on alway!
I wat we'll sail about the warld
   Until the Judgment Day."

Noah sent a doo far owre the sea,
   It flew into the south.
It stayed four days and cam again
   Wi' a leaf within its mouth.

Noah sent a doo far owre the sea,
   It to the wast is ta'en.
It tarried late, it tarried lang,
   And cam'na back again.

"O what's yon green hill in the wast
   Set round wi' mony a tree?"
"I wat it is Mount Ararat
   New risen frae the sea."

He's set the Ark for Ararat,
   He's plied her owre the faem,
He's lighted down at Ararat,
   And there he's made his hame.

Variations on a Time Theme

1934

*

And another king shall rise after them . . .
and think that he may change times and
laws, and they shall be given into his hands,
until a time, and times, and dividing of times

I

After the fever this long convalescence,
Chapped blood and growing pains, waiting for life,
Turning away from hope, too dull for speculation.

How did we come here to this broken wood?
Splintered stumps, flapping bark, ringwormed boles,
Soft milk-white water prisoned in jagged holes
Like gaps where tusks have been.
                        Where did the road branch?
Where did the path turn like an enemy turning
Stealthily, suddenly, showing his other face
After the knife-stroke?
                  Or did we choose, and if we chose
Did we choose idly, following the fawning way,
Or after years of obstinate dubitation,
Night sweats, rehearsed refusals, choose at last
For only the choice was left?
                     Did we come here
Through darkness or inexplicable light,
The road all clear behind us and before us,
An answer and a riddle?
                Was it truth
That lured us here, or falsehood? Virtue itself,
Or weakness on weakness, an open stanchless wound?
Did we fight step by step, hacking our way
Through rank green flourishing hopes to come to this?

We did not know life held a place like this,
Or not for us, for others.
                  Yet we saw
Good halting stations on our road here, open doors,
Lights in windows, lighted shrines, and human faces
Not such as these.

We have seen Heaven opening,
And fields and souls in radiance. We have walked
In radiance and in darkness. Now this twilight.

Can we build a house here, make friends with the
    mangled stumps
And splintered stones, not looking too closely
At one another?
                    Can we sing our songs here,
Pray, lift a shrine to some god? Can we till these
    nameless fields,
Nameless ourselves, between the impotent dead
And the unborn, cut off from both, fateless,
Yet ruled by fate? Many will follow us.

II

At the dead centre of the boundless plain
Does our way end? Our horses pace and pace
Like steeds for ever labouring on a shield,
Keeping their solitary heraldic courses.

Our horses move on such a ground, for them
Perhaps the progress is all ease and pleasure,
But it is heavy work for us, the riders,
Whose hearts have flown so far ahead they are lost
    Long past all finding
While we sit staring at the same horizon.

Time has such curious stretches, we are told,
And generation after generation
May travel them, sad stationary journey,
Of what device, what meaning?

40

                              Yet these coursers
Have seen all and will see all. Suppliantly
The rocks will melt, the sealed horizons fall
Before their onset—and the places
Our hearts have hid in will be viewed by strangers
Sitting where we are, breathing the foreign air
Of the new realm they have inherited.
But we shall fall here on the plain.

                                    It may be
These steeds would stumble and the long road end
(So legend says) if they should lack their riders.
        But then a rider
Is always easy to find. Yet we fill a saddle
At least. We sit where others have sat before us
And others will sit after us.

                    It cannot be
These animals know their riders, mark the change
When one makes way for another. It cannot be
They know this wintry wilderness from spring.
For they have come from regions dreadful past
All knowledge. They have borne upon their saddles
Forms fiercer than the tiger, borne them calmly
As they bear us now.

                    And so we do not hope
That their great coal-black glossy hides
Should keep a glimmer of the autumn light
We still remember, when our limbs were weightless
As red leaves on a tree, and our silvery breaths
Went on before us like new-risen souls
Leading our empty bodies through the air.
A princely dream. Now all that golden country
Is razed as bare as Troy. We cannot return,
And shall not see the kingdom of our heirs.

41

These beasts are mortal, and we who fall so lightly,
Fall so heavily, are, it is said, immortal.
Such knowledge should armour us against all change,
And this monotony. Yet these worn saddles
Have powers to charm us to obliviousness.
They were appointed for us, and the scent of the
    ancient leather
Is strong as a spell. So we must mourn or rejoice
For this our station, our inheritance
As if it were all. This plain all. This journey all.

III

A child in Adam's field I dreamed away
My one eternity and hourless day,
Ere from my wrist Time's bird had learned to fly,
Or I had robbed the Tree of which I die,
Whose boughs rain still, whose fruit wave-green
    shall fall
Until the last great autumn reddens all.
Thence lured by demons or by angels driven,
A lonely shaft loosed from the bow's calm heaven,
Blind as an arrow I sped upon my race
And swiftly reached the sole remaining place,
My first and last since then. There soon I found
My restless home, my heaven, my hell, my ground,
And that to these allegiance I might vow,
Took quick the bloody sign upon my brow,
Fell Edenwards in innocent Abel slain
And rose twice-armoured in the flesh of Cain.
Thus harnessed, thus baptized, I now could go
Unscathed through my confederate crowd and show
The badge the world likes best. Till came the river
That scoured the world blind, and sunk for ever,

Drowned in ten thousand shapes I lay, though still
My only flesh no shame nor loss could kill
Rode on the flood to Ararat's safe hill.

Thenceforth oblivious of Heaven's foundered ship,
A youthful Abraham with bearded lip,
I walked the shrunken hills and clouded plains
Among my flocks, pleased with a shepherd's gains,
A shepherd's joys, not yet too wild or proud
For a small Eden in a wandering cloud.
Alas! no heavenly voice the passing told
Of that last Eden; my own bliss I sold.
Weary of being one, myself conspired
Against myself and into bondage hired
My mortal birthright. On dark Egypt's brow
As at the world's great helm behold me now,
Highest among the fallen, a man's length more
From what I sought than I had been before.

As he who snatches all at last will crave
To be of all there is the quivering slave,
So I from base to base slipped headlong down
Till all that glory was my mountainous crown.
Set free, or outlawed, now I walk the sand
And search this rubble for the promised land.

IV

Now at the road's quick turn
The enemy stands like a tower. The serpent rears
Its crest in blindness and light. Time dies
Its minute death, stiffens, moves on again.
The heroes march out to the unknown field.
The veterans return, bearing in feeble hands

43

The peace that is won and lost. The peasants
Climb the path in the rain to the mountain church.
The priest prays. The panting messenger
Falls by the way, his eyes and thoughts set onward,
And arm rigid. The prophet dreams on the peak.
The ark is borne unseen through the wilderness.

V

The infidel congregation of mankind
Flap sullenly upon the grinding storm,
Slow-motion flight over a bottomless road,
Or clinical fantasy begotten by
The knife of demon Time the vivisector
Incising nightmares.

                                Yet I thought they moved.

Or can it be this ground that heaves about them
Its giant mole-hills, lengthening league by league
The ghastly thin anatomy of Space Time
Stripped to the nerve?

                                There's nothing human here
To entertain these wraiths but night and day
Saluting them, and spring opening their hearts
To emptiness, and autumn shutting their hearts
On emptiness, stirring their hearts, not them.
The scenery summer shifts around them is
Dusty and frayed, and winter is a floor,
Swept and polished, where the devils weave
Their dance more cleanly and more honestly.

Once there were ancient cities here, and shrines
That branched from Adam's world.

44

                              Now these dead stones
Among dead stones, where the late nomads pitch
Their nightly tents, leaving a little refuse,
The comfortless smell of casual habitation,
Human or bestial—indistinguishable.
These; and light and water casting back
Our shallow masks to shame us. Or at most
The shades of our ancestors, lingering yet,
Play in the ruins of their former house,
Remembering the eyes once bent upon them
That one day left them.

                              That is long ago;
A memory of our fathers. We have known
Only this debris not yet overgrown,
Never to be removed.
                              Dead and our own.

                              VI

                    Forty years this burning
                    Circuitous path, feet spurning
                    The sliding sand and turning
                        The wheel, turning again
                    Sharp rock, soft dust, a land
                        Choked in sand.

                    Once in the wilderness
            A stream leapt from the smitten rock, flowed on,
                        flowed on, and then
                    The rock was sealed again,
                        Our hearts were dry again.
            Since then we have marched through emptiness
            Over the sea-ground of the sealess plain.

                                  45

To Sinai's hill one day
Jehovah came. His way
Was silent; silence rested
On the bright cloud, the bright and shadowy hill.
The rocks where the wild-birds nested
With glittering eyes were still.

The stream light-winding from His secret throne
Spoke to itself and was its own.
Till silence, come too near,
Grew loud and turned to fear.
We made a golden toy, with idle sound
Shattered the peace, and danced, and spurned the
sacred ground.
At evening Moses came
Down from the Mount bearing the Law and saw our
shame,
The brazen calf, the naked youths and men,
And broke the tables of the law again.
The wilderness has been our home since then.

All that is now a memory,
Burning, burning,
With Pharaoh's body floating on the sea
Among his wide-robed seers, his men and cavalry,
And the dim desert slowly turning,
And the evening shadows
On temple-mirroring Nile, the wells and shining
meadows.

We have passed great kingdoms by
In a separate dream.
Have seen tame birds wheel homing through the sky,
And towers caught in a distant gleam,
And smelt the searching scent of roots, the
moist and dry,

46

And stopped remembering,
In this hard torrid winter without spring,
Something once tender and green,
But wakening we have seen,
At the waste's ruined bounds,
Pale whirlwinds racing round like spectral hounds
And falling through the air with whispering sounds.

And we have loved these lonely shapes
At their disconsolate play,
Have looked up to the stony capes
Battered with scalding surf of sand
Like sailors watching after many a day
Their home hills rising from the spray.
Where is our land?

There is a stream
We have been told of. Where it is
We do not know. But it is not a dream,
Though like a dream. We cannot miss
The road that leads us to it. Fate
Will take us there that keeps us here.
Neither hope nor fear
Can hasten or retard the date
Of our deliverance; when we shall leave this sand
And enter the unknown and feared and longed-for
land.

VII

Ransomed from darkness and released in Time,
Caught, pinioned, blinded, sealed and cased in Time;
Summoned, elected, armed and crowned by Time,
Tried and condemned, stripped and disowned by Time;

Suckled and weaned, plumped and full-fed by Time,
Defrauded, starved, physicked and bled by Time;
Buried alive and buried dead by Time:

If there's no crack or chink, no escape from Time,
No spasm, no murderous knife to rape from Time
The pure and trackless day of liberty;
If there's no power can burst the rock of Time,
No Rescuer from the dungeon stock of Time,
Nothing in earth or heaven to set us free:
Imprisonment's for ever; we're the mock of Time,
While lost and empty lies Eternity.

VIII

Time's armies are the seconds soft as rain,
Whose wound's so fine it leaves no scar nor stain,
Whose feathery arrows rankle in my heart,
Yet are so light, though each a mortal dart,
That like Sebastian in the picture I
Can watch vicarious battles in the sky,
While this cruel plumage, stagy and absurd,
Of a plucked angel or half-naked bird,
Betrays my state to all eyes but my own.
Or I'm like Socrates at Marathon,
An absent hero with a pensive sword,
Ears cocked for his wise daimon's lightest word
Touching the scene, the cast, the spurious play,
The Gods and Time, while Time brings down the day
Like a great wrestler, fells it like a tree
With all its fruit, defeat or victory.

What though? All strategy here is plain retreat,
And the sure issue of this war defeat.

See, at the thought these arrow pricks grow sharper!
Oh, Plato himself was only Time's poor harper
Playing to bid him pause, Shakespeare a wile
To make him turn his head and once beguile
His wolfish heart. I know where ends the course,
And there my body like a headstrong horse
Will bear me without stop or hindrance. There
These archers will surround me quite, the air
Turn to a sea of feathers, and all art
End in a new yet long-foresuffered smart.

Time is a sea. There, if I could but sail
For ever and outface Death's bullying gale
I'd ask no more. From that great pond I'd fish
At pleasure every poet's and conqueror's wish.
The treasure of that deep's unbattened hold
I'd rifle clean till it and I were old,
And of that salvage worlds on worlds would make
Newer than tarried for Columbus' sake.
Until I dream, in that vast more and more,
I'd find Eternity's unhidden shore,
And the Gods, so old, so young, I'd not know which,
And Time between shrink to a shallow ditch.
Each wish is traitorous and a dupe the wisher.
It is not I but Time that is the fisher.
Me he will catch and stuff into his net
With mortal sweepings, harp and banneret.
He'll dredge the very heavens; dull stars will rust
Among my own and miscellaneous dust,
Light dust of fame that floats, heavy that sinks
Into this drunken sea that drinks and drinks.

Time's a fire-wheel whose spokes the seasons turn,
And fastened there we, Time's slow martyrs, burn.
To some that rage is but a pleasant heat,

And the red fiery bower as summer sweet.
Others there are who lord it in the flame,
And, while they're burning, dice for power and fame.
A choicer company ignore the pyre,
And dream and prophesy amid the fire.
And a few with eyes uplifted through the blaze
Let their flesh crumble till they're all a gaze
Glassing that fireless kingdom in the sky
Which is our dream as through Time's wood we fly
Burning in silence or crying the ancient rhyme:
'Who shall outsoar the mountainous flame of Time?'

IX

Packed in my skin from head to toe
Is one I know and do not know.
He never speaks to me yet is at home
More snug than embryo in the womb.
His lodgings are but poor; they neither please
Nor irk him greatly, though he sees
Their cracks, rents, flaws, impossibilities
As in a glass. He is safe, he has no doubt,
He sits secure and will not out.

His name's Indifference.
Nothing offending he is all offence;
Can stare at beauty's bosom coldly
And at Christ's crucifixion boldly;
Can note with a lack-lustre eye
Victim and murderer go by;
Can pore upon the maze of lust
And watch the lecher fall to dust
With the same glance; content can wait
By a green bank near Eden's gate

To see the first blood flow and see naught then
Except a bright and glittering rain.
If I could drive this demon out
I'd put all Time's display to rout.
Its wounds would turn to flowers and nothing be
But the first Garden. The one Tree
Would stand for ever safe and fair
And Adam's hand stop in the air.
Or so I dream when at my door
I hear my Soul, my Visitor.

He comes but seldom and I cannot tell
If he's myself or one that loves me well
And comes in pity, for he pities all:
Weeps for the hero's and the beggar's fall;
The conqueror before his fallen foe
(Fingering his useless sword he cannot go,
But stands in doltish silence, unappeased);
Bereavement that, by deathless memory teased,
Pores on the same for-ever-altered track,
Turns, always on the old blind way turns back;
Lost Love that flies aghast it knows not where
And finds no foothold but the dreadful air;
The unending open wound in Jesus' side;
And all that has to die and that has died.

Pity would cancel what it feeds upon,
And gladly cease, its office done.
Yet could it end all passion, flaw, offence,
Would come my homespun fiend Indifference
And have me wholly. On these double horns
I take my comfort, they're my truckle bed;
Could Pity change the crown of thorns
To roses peace would soon be fled,
And I would have no place to rest my head.

Then must dead Pity, quickened by my plight,
Start up again and make for my delight
A mimic stage where all the day
A phantom hound pursues a phantom prey,
Where the slain rise and smile upon the slayer,
And the crowned victor is a harmless player,
And cunning is a fond deceit,
Treachery feigned and loss imaginary,
And friends consent to meet
To stage a slaughter and make up a story.

Oh, then, at such deceitful art,
Tears, real and burning, from my lids would start,
And peace would burst into my heart.

X

Who curbed the lion long ago
And penned him in this towering field
And reared him wingless in the sky?
And quenched the dragon's burning eye,
Chaining him here to make a show,
The faithful guardian of the shield?

A fabulous wave far back in Time
Flung these calm trophies to this shore
That looks out on a different sea.
These relics of a buried war,
Empty as shape and cold as rhyme,
Gaze now on fabulous wars to be.

So well the storm must have fulfilled
Its task of perfect overthrow
That this new world to them must seem
Irrecognizably the same,

And looking from the flag and shield
They see the self-same road they know.

Here now heraldic watch them ride
This path far up the mountain-side
And backward never cast a look;
Ignorant that the dragon died
Long since and that the mountain shook
When the great lion was crucified.

Journeys and Places

1937

Here at my earthly station set,
The revolutions of the year
Bear me bound and only let
This astronomic world appear.

Yet if I could reverse my course
Through ever-deepening yesterday,
Retrace the path that led me here,
Could I find a different way?

I would see eld's frosted hair
Burn black again and passion rage
On to its source and die away
At last in childhood's tranquil age.

Charlemagne's death-palsied hand
Would move once more and never rest,
Until by deadlier weakness bound
It lay against his mother's breast.

Saint Augustine gives back his soul
To stumble in the endless maze.
After Jesus Venus stands
In the centre of his gaze,

While still from death to life to naught
Gods, dynasties, and nations flit;
Though for a while among the sand
Unchanged the changing Pharaohs sit.

Fast the horizons empty. Now
Nothing's to see but wastes and rocks,
And on the thinning Asian plains
A few wild shepherds with their flocks . . .

So, back or forward, still we strike
   Through time and touch its dreaded goal.
Eternity's the fatal flaw
   Through which run out world, life and soul.

And there in transmutation's blank
   No mortal mind has ever read,
Or told what soul and shape are, there,
   Blue wave, red rose, and Plato's head.

For there Immortal Being in
   Solidity more pure than stone
Sleeps through the circle, pillar, arch,
   Spiral, cone, and pentagon.

To the mind's eternity I turn,
   With leaf, fruit, blossom on the spray,
See the dead world grow green within
   Imagination's one long day.

There while outstretched upon the Tree
   Christ looks across Jerusalem's towers,
Adam and Eve unfallen yet
   Sleep side by side within their bowers.

There while fast in the Roman snare
   The Carthaginian thinks of home,
A boy carefree in Carthage streets,
   Hannibal fights a little Rome,

David and Homer tune their harps,
   Gaza is up, sprung from its wreck,
Samson goes free, Delilah's shears
   Join his strong ringlets to his neck.

A dream! the astronomic years
   Patrolled by stars and planets bring
Time led in chains from post to post
   Of the all-conquering Zodiac ring.

THE MOUNTAINS

The days have closed behind my back
   Since I came into these hills.
Now memory is a single field
   One peasant tills and tills.

So far away, if I should turn
   I know I could not find
That place again. These mountains make
   The backward gaze half-blind,

Yet sharp my sight till it can catch
   The ranges rising clear
Far in futurity's high-walled land;
   But I am rooted here.

And do not know where lies my way,
   Backward or forward. If I could
I'd leap time's bound or turn and hide
   From time in my ancestral wood.

Double delusion! Here I'm held
   By the mystery of the rock,
Must watch in a perpetual dream
   The horizon's gates unlock and lock,

See on the harvest fields of time
  The mountains heaped like sheaves,
And the valleys opening out
  Like a volume's turning leaves,

Dreaming of a peak whose height
  Will show me every hill,
A single mountain on whose side
  Life blooms for ever and is still.

THE HILL

And turning north around the hill,
The flat sea like an adder curled,
And a flat rock amid the sea
That gazes towards the ugly town,
And on the sands, flat and brown,
A thousand naked bodies hurled
Like an army overthrown.

And turning south around the hill,
Fields flowering in the curling waves,
And shooting from the white sea-walls
Like a thousand waterfalls,
Rapturous divers never still.
Motion and gladness. O this hill
Was made to show these cliffs and caves.

So he thought. But he has never
Stood again upon that hill.
He lives far inland by a river
That somewhere else divides these lands,
But where or how he does not know,

Or where the countless pathways go
That turn and turn to reach the sea
On this or that side of the hill,
Or if, arriving, he will be
With the bright divers never still,
Or on the sad dishonoured sands.

THE ROAD

There is a road that turning always
    Cuts off the country of Again.
Archers stand there on every side
    And as it runs time's deer is slain,
    And lies where it has lain.

That busy clock shows never an hour.
    All flies and all in flight must tarry.
The hunter shoots the empty air
    Far on before the quarry,
    Which falls though nothing's there to parry.

The lion crouching in the centre
    With mountain head and sunset brow
Rolls down the everlasting slope
    Bones picked an age ago,
    And the bones rise up and go.

There the beginning finds the end
    Before beginning ever can be,
And the great runner never leaves
    The starting and the finishing tree,
    The budding and the fading tree.

There the ship sailing safe in harbour
   Long since in many a sea was drowned.
The treasure burning in her hold
   So near will never be found,
   Sunk past all sound.

There a man on a summer evening
   Reclines at ease upon his tomb
And is his mortal effigy.
   And there within the womb,
   The cell of doom,

The ancestral deed is thought and done,
   And in a million Edens fall
A million Adams drowned in darkness,
   For small is great and great is small,
   And a blind seed all.

THE MYTHICAL JOURNEY

First in the North. The black sea-tangle beaches,
Brine-bitter stillness, tablet-strewn morass,
Tall women against the sky with heads covered,
The witch's house below the black-toothed mountain,
Wave-echo in the roofless chapel,
The twice-dead castle on the swamp-green mound,
Darkness at noon-day, wheel of fire at midnight,
The level sun and the wild shooting shadows.

How long ago? Then sailing up to summer
Over the edge of the world. Black hill of water,
Rivers of running gold. The sun! The sun!
Then the free summer isles.
But the ship hastened on and brought him to
The towering walls of life and the great kingdom.

Where long he wandered seeking that which sought him
Through all the little hills and shallow valleys.
One whose form and features,
Race and speech he did not know, shapeless, tongueless,
Known to him only by the impotent heart,
And whether at all on earth the place of meeting,
Beyond all knowledge. Only the little hills,
Head-high, and the winding valleys,
Turning, returning, till there grew a pattern,
And it was held. And there stood both in their stations
With the hills between them. And that was the meaning.

Though sometimes through the wavering light and shadow
He thought he saw it a moment as he watched
The red deer walking by the riverside
At evening, when the bells were ringing,
And the bright stream leapt silent from the mountain
Far in the sunset. But as he looked, nothing
Was there but lights and shadows.

                        And then the vision
Of the conclusion without fulfilment.
The plain of glass and in the crystal grave
That which he had sought, that which had sought him,
Glittering in death. And all the dead scattered
Like fallen stars, clustered like leaves hanging
From the sad boughs of the mountainous tree of Adam
Planted far down in Eden. And on the hills
The gods reclined and conversed with each other
From summit to summit.

                              Conclusion
Without fulfilment. Thence the dream rose upward,
The living dream sprung from the dying vision,
Overarching all. Beneath its branches
He builds in faith and doubt his shaking house.

TRISTRAM'S JOURNEY

He strode across the room and flung
   The letter down: 'You need not tell
Your treachery, harlot!' He was gone
   Ere Iseult fainting fell.

He rode out from Tintagel gate,
   He heard his charger slowly pace,
And ever hung a cloud of gnats
   Three feet before his face.

At a wood's border he turned round
   And saw the distant castle side,
Iseult looking towards the wood,
   Mark's window gaping wide.

He turned again and slowly rode
   Into the forest's flickering shade,
And now as sunk in waters green
   Were armour, helm, and blade.

First he awoke with night around
   And heard the wind, and woke again
At noon within a ring of hills,
   At sunset on a plain.

And hill and plain and wood and tower
   Passed on and on and turning came
Back to him, tower and wood and hill,
   Now different, now the same.

There was a castle on a lake.
   The castle doubled in the mere
Confused him, his uncertain eye
   Wavered from there to here.

A window in the wall had held
    Iseult upon a summer day,
While he and Palomide below
    Circled in furious fray.

But now he searched the towers, the sward,
    And struggled something to recall,
A stone, a shadow. Blank the lake,
    And empty every wall.

He left his horse, left sword and mail,
    And went into the woods and tore
The branches from the clashing trees
    Until his rage was o'er.

And now he wandered on the hills
    In peace. Among the shepherd's flocks
Often he lay so long, he seemed
    One of the rocks.

The shepherds called and made him run
    Like a tame cur to round the sheep.
At night he lay among the dogs
    Beside a well to sleep.

And he forgot Iseult and all.
    Dagonet once and two came by
Like tall escutcheoned animals
    With antlers towering high.

He snapped their spears, rove off their helms,
    And beat them with his hands and sent
Them onward with a bitter heart,
    But knew not where they went.

They came to Mark and told him how
  A madman ruled the hinds and kept
The wandering sheep. Mark haled him to
  Tintagel while he slept.

He woke and saw King Mark at chess
  And Iseult with her maids at play,
The arras where the scarlet knights
  And ladies stood all day.

None knew him. In the garden once
  Iseult walked in the afternoon,
Her hound leapt up and licked his face,
  Iseult fell in a swoon.

There as he leaned the misted grass
  Cleared blade by blade below his face,
The round walls hardened as he looked,
  And he was in his place.

HÖLDERLIN'S JOURNEY

When Hölderlin started from Bordeaux
  He was not mad but lost in mind,
For time and space had fled away
  With her he had to find.

'The morning bells rang over France
  From tower to tower. At noon I came
Into a maze of little hills,
  Head-high and every hill the same.

'A little world of emerald hills,
   And at their heart a faint bell tolled;
Wedding or burial, who could say?
   For death, unseen, is bold.

'Too small to climb, too tall to show
   More than themselves, the hills lay round.
Nearer to her, or farther? They
   Might have stretched to the world's bound.

'A shallow candour was their all,
   And the mean riddle, How to tally
Reality with such appearance,
   When in the nearest valley

'Perhaps already she I sought,
   She, sought and seeker, had gone by,
And each of us in turn was trapped
   By simple treachery.

'The evening brought a field, a wood.
   I left behind the hills of lies,
And watched beside a mouldering gate
   A deer with its rock-crystal eyes.

'On either pillar of the gate
   A deer's head watched within the stone.
The living deer with quiet look
   Seemed to be gazing on

'Its pictured death—and suddenly
   I knew, Diotima was dead,
As if a single thought had sprung
   From the cold and the living head.

'That image held me and I saw
      All moving things so still and sad,
But till I came into the mountains
      I know I was not mad.

'What made the change? The hills and towers
      Stood otherwise than they should stand,
And without fear the lawless roads
      Ran wrong through all the land.

'Upon the swarming towns of iron
      The bells hailed down their iron peals,
Above the iron bells the swallows
      Glided on iron wheels.

'And there I watched in one confounded
      The living and the unliving head.
Why should it be? For now I know
      Diotima was dead

'Before I left the starting place;
      Empty the course, the garland gone,
And all that race as motionless
      As these two heads of stone.'

So Hölderlin mused for thirty years
      On a green hill by Tübingen,
Dragging in pain a broken mind
      And giving thanks to God and men.

THE FALL

What shape had I before the Fall?
      What hills and rivers did I seek?
What were my thoughts then? And of what
      Forgotten histories did I speak

68

To my companions? Did our eyes
  From their foredestined watching-place
See Heaven and Earth one land, and range
  Therein through all of Time and Space?

Did I see Chaos and the Word,
  The suppliant Dust, the moving Hand,
Myself, the Many and the One,
  The dead, the living Land?

That height cannot be scaled again.
  My fall was like the fall that burst
Old Lear's heart on the summer sward.
  Where I lie now I stood at first.

The ancient pain returns anew.
  Where was I ere I came to man?
What shape among the shapes that once
  Agelong through endless Eden ran?

Did I see there the dragon brood
  By streams their emerald scales unfold,
While from their amber eyeballs fell
  Soft-rayed the rustling gold?

It must be that one time I walked
  By rivers where the dragon drinks;
But this side Eden's wall I meet
  On every twisting road the Sphinx

Whose head is like a wooden prow
  That forward leaning dizzily
Over the seas of whitened worlds
  Has passed and nothing found to see,

Whose breast, a flashing ploughshare, once
    Cut the rich furrows wrinkled in
Venusberg's sultry underworld
    And busy trampled fields of sin,

Whose salt-white brow like crusted fire
    Smiles ever, whose cheeks are red as blood,
Whose dolphin back is flowered yet
    With wrack that swam upon the Flood.

Since then in antique attitudes
    I swing the bright two-handed sword
And strike and strike the marble brow,
    Wide-eyed and watchful as a bird,

Smite hard between the basilisk eyes,
    And carve the snaky dolphin side,
Until the coils are cloven in two
    And free the glittering pinions glide.

Like quicksilver the scales slip down,
    Upon the air the spirit flies,
And so I build me Heaven and Hell
    To buy my bartered Paradise.

While from a legendary height
    I see a shadowy figure fall,
And not far off another beats
    With his bare hands on Eden's wall.

TROY

He all that time among the sewers of Troy
Scouring for scraps. A man so venerable
He might have been Priam's self, but Priam was dead,
Troy taken. His arms grew meagre as a boy's,
And all that flourished in that hollow famine
Was his long, white, round beard. Oh, sturdily
He swung his staff and sent the bold rats skipping
Across the scurfy hills and worm-wet valleys,
Crying: 'Achilles, Ajax, turn and fight!
Stop cowards!' Till his cries, dazed and confounded,
Flew back at him with: 'Coward, turn and fight!'
And the wild Greeks yelled round him.
Yet he withstood them, a brave, mad old man,
And fought the rats for Troy. The light was rat-grey,
The hills and dells, the common drain, his Simois,
Rat-grey. Mysterious shadows fell
Affrighting him whenever a cloud offended
The sun up in the other world. The rat-hordes,
Moving, were grey dust shifting in grey dust.
Proud history has such sackends. He was taken
At last by some chance robber seeking treasure
Under Troy's riven roots. Dragged to the surface.
And there he saw Troy like a burial ground
With tumbled walls for tombs, the smooth sward wrinkled
As Time's last wave had long since passed that way,
The sky, the sea, Mount Ida and the islands,
No sail from edge to edge, the Greeks clean gone.
They stretched him on a rock and wrenched his limbs,
Asking: 'Where is the treasure?' till he died.

A TROJAN SLAVE

I've often wandered in the fields of Troy
Beneath the walls, seen Paris as a boy
Before youth made him vicious. Hector's smile
And untried lion-look can still beguile
My heart of peace. That was before the fall,
When high still stood Troy's many-tunnelled wall.
Now I am shackled to a Grecian dolt,
Pragmatic, race-proud as a pampered colt.
All here is strange to me, the country kings,
This cold aspiring race, the mountain-rings
On every side. They are like toppling snow-wreaths
Heaped on Troy's hearth. Yet still an ember breathes
Below to breed its crop of yearly ills,
The flowering trees on the unreal hills.
These bring Troy back. And when along the stone
The lizard flickers, thirty years I'm thrown
At odds and stand again where once I stood,
And see Troy's towers burn like a winter wood.
For then into their country all in flame,
From their uncounted caves the lizards came
And looked and melted in a glaze of fire,
While all the wall quivered and sang like wire
As heat ate all. I saw calamity
In action there, and it will always be
Before me in the lizard on the stone.
  But in my heart a deeper spite has grown,
This, that they would not arm us, and preferred
Troy's ruin lest a slave should snatch a sword
And fight even at their side. Yet in that fall
They lost no more than we who lost our all.
Troy was our breath, our soul, and all our wit,
Who did not own it but were owned by it.
We must have fought for Troy. We were its hands,

72

And not like those mere houses, flocks, and lands.
We were the Trojans; they at best could swell
A pompous or a bloody spectacle.
And so we watched with dogs outside the ring
Heroes fall cheap as meat, king slaughtering king
Like fatted cattle. Yet they did not guess
How our thoughts wantoned with their wantonness.
They were too high for that; they guessed too late,
When full had grown our knowledge and our hate.
And then they thought, with arms as strong as theirs,
We too might make a din with swords and spears,
And while they feared the Greeks they feared us most,
And ancient Troy was lost and we were lost.

Now an old man—why should that one regret,
When all else has grown tranquil, shake me yet?
Of all my life I know one thing, I know,
Before I was a slave, long, long ago,
I lost a sword in a forgotten fight,
And ever since my arm has been too light
For this dense world, and shall grow lighter still.
Yet through that rage shines Troy's untroubled hill,
And many a tumbled wall and vanished tree
Remains, as if in spite, a happy memory.

MERLIN

O Merlin in your crystal cave
Deep in the diamond of the day,
Will there ever be a singer
Whose music will smooth away
The furrow drawn by Adam's finger
Across the meadow and the wave?

Or a runner who'll outrun
Man's long shadow driving on,
Break through the gate of memory
And hang the apple on the tree?
Will your magic ever show
The sleeping bride shut in her bower,
The day wreathed in its mound of snow
And Time locked in his tower?

THE ENCHANTED KNIGHT

Lulled by La Belle Dame Sans Merci he lies
  In the bare wood below the blackening hill.
The plough drives nearer now, the shadow flies
  Past him across the plain, but he lies still.

Long since the rust its gardens here has planned,
  Flowering his armour like an autumn field.
From his sharp breast-plate to his iron hand
  A spider's web is stretched, a phantom shield.

When footsteps pound the turf beside his ear
  Armies pass through his dream in endless line,
And one by one his ancient friends appear;
  They pass all day, but he can make no sign.

When a bird cries within the silent grove
  The long-lost voice goes by, he makes to rise
And follow, but his cold limbs never move,
  And on the turf unstirred his shadow lies.

But if a withered leaf should drift
  Across his face and rest, the dread drops start
Chill on his forehead. Now he tries to lift
  The insulting weight that stays and breaks his heart.

MARY STUART

My brother Jamie lost me all,
Fell cleverly to make me fall,
And with a sure reluctant hand
Stole my life and took my land.

It was jealousy of the womb
That let me in and shut him out,
Honesty, kingship, all shut out,
While I enjoyed the royal room.

My father was his, but not my mother,
We were, yet were not, sister, brother,
To reach my mother he had to strike
Me down and leap that deadly dyke.

Over the wall I watched him move
At ease through all the guarded grove,
Then hack, and hack, and hack it down,
Until that ruin was his own.

IBSEN

Sollness climbs the dwindling tower
      And all the hills fall flat.
Hilda Wangel down below
      Now is no bigger than her hat.

Sollness steps into the air,
      All Norway lies below him, Brand
Frowning on the rusty heath,
      Peer's half-witted fairyland,

Nora stumbling from a door,
　　Hedda burning a book,
Doctor Stockman fishing up
　　Bacilli from the brook,

Rebecca circling in the weir,
　　The Rat Wife whipping round a wall;
The Pillars of Society
　　Fall thundering with his fall.

And flashing by his house he sees it
　　Split from earth to sky,
And his wife and children sitting
　　Naked to every passer-by.

THE TOWN BETRAYED

Our homes are eaten out by time,
　　Our lawns strewn with our listless sons,
Our harlot daughters lean and watch
　　The ships crammed down with shells and guns.

Like painted prows far out they lean:
　　A world behind, a world before.
The leaves are covering up our hills,
　　Neptune has locked the shore.

Our yellow harvests lie forlorn
　　And there we wander like the blind,
Returning from the golden field
　　With famine in our mind.

Far inland now the glittering swords
  In order rise, in order fall,
In order on the dubious field
  The dubious trumpets call.

Yet here there is no word, no sign
  But quiet murder in the street.
Our leaf-light lives are spared or taken
  By men obsessed and neat.

We stand beside our windows, see
  In order dark disorder come,
And prentice killers duped by death
  Bring and not know our doom.

Our cattle wander at their will.
  To-day a horse pranced proudly by.
The dogs run wild. Vultures and kites
  Wait in the towers for us to die.

At evening on the parapet
  We sit and watch the sun go down,
Reading the landscape of the dead,
  The sea, the hills, the town.

There our ancestral ghosts are gathered.
  Fierce Agamemnon's form I see,
Watching as if his tents were time
  And Troy eternity.

We must take order, bar our gates,
  Fight off these phantoms. Inland now
Achilles, Siegfried, Lancelot
  Have sworn to bring us low.

THE UNFAMILIAR PLACE

I do not know this place,
Though here for long I have run
My changing race
In the moon and the sun,
Within this wooded glade
Far up the mountainside
Where Christ and Caesar died
And the first man was made.

I have seen this turning light
For many a day.
I have not been away
Even in dreams of the night.
In the unnumbered names
My fathers gave these things
I seek a kingdom lost,
Sleeping with folded wings.
I have questioned many a ghost
Far inland in my dreams,
Enquired of fears and shames
The dark and winding way
To the day within my day.

And aloft I have stood
And given my eyes their fill,
Have watched the bad and the good
Go up and down the hill,
The peasants on the plain
Ploughing the fields red,
The roads running alone,
The ambush in the wood,
The victim walking on,
The misery-blackened door

That never will open again,
The tumblers at the fair,
The watchers on the stair,
Cradle and bridal-bed,
The living and the dead
Scattered on every shore.

All this I have seen
Twice over, there and here,
Knocking at dead men's gates
To ask the living way,
And viewing this upper scene.
But I am balked by fear
And what my lips say
To drown the voice of fear.
The earthly day waits.

THE PLACE OF LIGHT AND DARKNESS

Walking on the harvest hills of Night
Time's elder brother, the great husbandman,
Goes on his ancient round. His massive lantern,
Simpler than the first fashion, lights the rows
Of stooks that lean like little golden graves
Or tasselled barges foundering low
In the black stream.
                          He sees that all is ready,
The trees all stripped, the orchards bare, the nests
Empty. All things grown
Homeless and whole. He sees the hills of grain,
A day all yellow and red, flowers, fruit, and corn.
The soft hair harvest-golden in darkness.
Children playing
In the late night-black day of time. He sees

The lover standing by the trysting-tree
Who'll never find his love till all are gathered
In light or darkness. The unnumbered living
Numbered and bound and sheaved.

                                    O could that day
Break on this side of time!

                                    A wind shakes
The loaded sheaves, the feathery tomb bursts open,
And yellow hair is poured along the ground
From the bent neck of time. The woods cry:
This is the resurrection.

O little judgment days lost in the dark,
Seen by the bat and screech-owl!

                                    He goes on,
Bearing within his ocean-heart the jewel,
The day all yellow and red wherein a sun
Shines on the endless harvest lands of time.

THE SOLITARY PLACE

O I shall miss
With one small breath these centuries
Of harvest-home uncounted!
I have known
The mead, the bread,
And the mounds of grain
As half my riches. But the fields will change,
And their harvest would be strange
If I could return. I should know again
Only the lint-white stubble plain
From which the summer-painted birds have flown
A year's life on.

But I can never
See with these eyes the double-threaded river
That runs through life and death and death and life,
Weaving one scene. Which I and not I
Blindfold have crossed, I and not I
Will cross again, my face, my feet, my hands
Gleaned from lost lands
To be sown again.

O certain prophecy,
And faithful tragedy,
Furnished with scenery of sorrow and strife,
The Cross and the Flood
And Babel's towers
And Abel's blood
And Eden's bowers,
Where I and not I
Lived and questioned and made reply:
None else to ask or make reply . . .

If there is none else to ask or reply
But I and not I,
And when I stretch out my hand my hand comes towards me
To pull me across to me and back to me,
If my own mind, questioning, answers me
And there is no other answer to me,
If all that I see,
Woman and man and beast and rock and sky,
Is a flat image shut behind an eye,
And only my thoughts can meet me or pass me or follow me,
O then I am alone,
I, many and many in one,
A lost player upon a hill
On a sad evening when the world is still,
The house empty, brother and sister gone
Beyond the reach of sight, or sound of any cry,
Into the bastion of the mind, behind the shutter of the eye.

THE PRIVATE PLACE

This stranger holding me from head to toe,
This deaf usurper I shall never know,
Who lives in household quiet in my unrest,
And of my troubles weaves his tranquil nest,
Who never smiles or frowns or bows his head,
And while I rage is insolent as the dead,
Composed, indifferent, thankless, faithful, he
Is my ally and only enemy.

Come then, take up the cleansing blade once more
That drives all difference out. The fabled shore
Sees us again. Now the predestined fight,
The ancestral stroke, the opening gash of light:
Side by side myself by myself slain,
The wakening stir, the eyes loaded with gain
Of ocean darkness, the rising hand in hand,
I with myself at one, the changed land,
My home, my country. But this precious seal
Will slowly crumble, the thief time will steal
Soft-footed bit by bit this boundless treasure
Held in four hands. I shall regain my measure,
My old measure again, shrink to a room, a shelf
Where decently I lay away myself,
Become the anxious warder, groan and fret
My thankless service to this martinet
Who sleeps and sleeps and rules. I hold this life
Only in strife and the aftertaste of strife
With this dull champion and thick-witted king.
But at one word he'll leap into the ring.

THE UNATTAINED PLACE

We have seen the world of good deeds spread
With its own sky above it
A length away
Our whole day,
Yet have not crossed from our false kindred.
We could have leapt straight from the womb to bliss
And never lost it after,
Been cradled, baptized, bred in that which is
And never known this frontier laughter,
But that we hate this place so much
And hating love it,
And that our weakness is such
That it must clutch
All weakness to it and can never release
The bound and battling hands,
The one hand bound, the other fighting
The fellow-foe it's tied to, righting
Weakness with weakness, rending, reuniting
The torn and incorruptible bands
That bind all these united and disunited lands,—
While there lies our predestined power and ease,
There, in those natural fields, life-fostering seas.

If we could be more weak
Than weakness' self, if we could break
This static hold with a mere blank, with nothing,
If we could take
Memory and thought and longing
Up by the roots and cast them behind our back,
If we could stop this ceaseless ringing and singing
That keeps our fingers flying in hate and love,
If we could cut off,
If we could unmake

What we were made to make:

But that we then should lose
Our loss,
Our kingdom's crown,
And to great Nothing toss
Our last left jewel down,
The light that long before us was,
The land we did not own,
The choice we could not choose.
For once we played upon that other hill,
And from that house we come.
There is a line around it still
And all inside is home.
Once there we pored on every stone and tree
In a long dream through the unsetting day,
And looking up could nothing see
But the right way on every way.
And lost it after,
No foot knows where,
To find this mourning air,
Commemorative laughter,
The mask, the doom
Written backwards,
The illegible tomb
Pointing backwards,
The reverse side
Where strength is weakness.
The body, pride,
The soul, a sickness.

Yet from that missing heaven outspread
Here all we read.

THE THREEFOLD PLACE

This is the place. The autumn field is bare,
  The row lies half-cut all the afternoon,
The birds are hiding in the woods, the air
  Dreams fitfully outworn with waiting.
                                        Soon

Out of the russet woods in amber mail
  Heroes come walking through the yellow sheaves,
Walk on and meet. And then a silent gale
  Scatters them on the field like autumn leaves.

Yet not a feathered stalk has stirred, and all
  Is still again, but for the birds that call
On every warrior's head and breast and shield.
  Sweet cries and horror on the field.

One field. I look again and there are three:
  One where the heroes fell to rest,
One where birds make of iron limbs a tree,
  Helms for a nest,
  And one where grain stands up like armies drest.

THE ORIGINAL PLACE

This is your native land.
By ancient inheritance
Your lives are free, though a hand
Strange to you set you here,
Ordained this liberty
And gave you hope and fear
And the turning maze of chance.

85

To weave our tale of Time
Rhyme is knit to rhyme
So close, it's like a proof
That nothing else can be
But this one tapestry
Where gleams under the woof
A giant Fate half-grown,
Imprisoned and its own.

To your unquestioned rule
No bound is set. You were
Made for this work alone.
This is your native air.
You could not leave these fields.
And when Time is grown
Beneath your countless hands
They say this kingdom shall
Be stable and beautiful.

But at its centre stands
A stronghold never taken,
Stormed at hourly in vain,
Held by a force unknown
That neither answers nor yields.
There our arms are shaken,
There the hero was slain
That bleeds upon our shields.

THE SUFFICIENT PLACE

See, all the silver roads wind in, lead in
To this still place like evening. See, they come
Like messengers bearing gifts to this little house,
And this great hill worn down to a patient mound,

And these tall trees whose motionless branches bear
An aeon's summer foliage, leaves so thick
They seem to have robbed a world of shade, and kept
No room for all these birds that line the boughs
With heavier riches, leaf and bird and leaf.
Within the doorway stand
Two figures, Man and Woman, simple and clear
As a child's first images. Their manners are
Such as were known before the earliest fashion
Taught the Heavens guile. The room inside is like
A thought that needed thus much space to write on,
Thus much, no more. Here all's sufficient. None
That comes complains, and all the world comes here,
Comes, and goes out again, and comes again.
This is the Pattern, these the Archetypes,
Sufficient, strong, and peaceful. All outside
From end to end of the world is tumult. Yet
These roads do not turn in here but writhe on
Round the wild earth for ever. If a man
Should chance to find this place three times in time
His eyes are changed and make a summer silence
Amid the tumult, seeing the roads wind in
To their still home, the house and the leaves and birds.

THE DREAMT-OF PLACE

I saw two towering birds cleaving the air
And thought they were Paolo and Francesca
Leading the lost, whose wings like silver billows
Rippled the azure sky from shore to shore,
They were so many. The nightmare god was gone
Who roofed their pain, the ghastly glen lay open,
The hissing lake was still, the fiends were fled,

And only some few headless, footless mists
Crawled out and in the iron-hearted caves.
Like light's unearthly eyes the lost looked down,
And heaven was filled and moving. Every height
On earth was thronged and all that lived stared upward.
I thought, This is the reconciliation,
This is the day after the Last Day,
The lost world lies dreaming within its coils,
Grass grows upon the surly sides of Hell,
Time has caught time and holds it fast for ever.
And then I thought, Where is the knife, the butcher,
The victim? Are they all here in their places?
Hid in this harmony? But there was no answer.

The Narrow Place

1943

TO J. F. H. (1897–1934)

Shot from the sling into the perilous road,
The hundred mile long hurtling bowling alley,
To-day I saw you pass full tilt for the jack.
Or it seemed a race beyond time's gate you rode,
Trussed to the motor cycle, shoulder and head
Fastened to flying fate, so that your back
Left nothing but a widening wake of dumb
Scornful oblivion. It was you, yet some
Soft finger somewhere turned a different day,
The day I left you in that narrow valley,
Close to my foot, but already far away;
And I remembered you were seven years dead.

Yet you were there so clearly, I could not tell
For a moment in the hot still afternoon
What world I walked in, since it held us two,
A dead and a living man. Had I cracked the shell
That hides the secret souls, had I fallen through,
I idly wondered, and in so falling found
The land where life's untraceable truants run
Hunting a halting stage? Was this the ground
That stretched beyond the span-wide world-wide ditch,
So like the ground I knew, yet so unlike,
Because it said 'Again', all this again,
The flying road, the motionless house again,
And, stretched between, the tension of your face—
As you ran in dust the burning comet's race
Athirst for the ease of ash—the eating itch
To be elsewhere, nowhere, the driving pain
Clamping the shoulders back? Was death's low dike
So easy to leap as this and so commonplace,
A jump from here through here straight into here,
An operation to make you what you were
Before, no better or worse? And yet the fear?

The clock-hand moved, the street slipped into its place,
Two cars went by. A chance face flying past
Had started it all and made a hole in space,
The hole you looked through always. I knew at last
The sight you saw there, the terror and mystery
Of unrepeatable life so plainly given
To you half wrapped still in eternity,
Who had come by such a simple road from heaven;
So that you did not need to have the story
Retold, or bid the heavy world turn again,
But felt the terror of the trysting place,
The crowning test, the treachery and the glory.

THE WAYSIDE STATION

Here at the wayside station, as many a morning,
I watch the smoke torn from the fumy engine
Crawling across the field in serpent sorrow.
Flat in the east, held down by stolid clouds,
The struggling day is born and shines already
On its warm hearth far off. Yet something here
Glimmers along the ground to show the seagulls
White on the furrows' black unturning waves.

But now the light has broadened.
I watch the farmstead on the little hill,
That seems to mutter: 'Here is day again'
Unwillingly. Now the sad cattle wake
In every byre and stall,
The ploughboy stirs in the loft, the farmer groans
And feels the day like a familiar ache
Deep in his body, though the house is dark.
The lovers part

Now in the bedroom where the pillows gleam
Great and mysterious as deep hills of snow,
An inaccessible land. The wood stands waiting
While the bright snare slips coil by coil around it,
Dark silver on every branch. The lonely stream
That rode through darkness leaps the gap of light,
Its voice grown loud, and starts its winding journey
Through the day and time and war and history.

THE RIVER

The silent stream flows on and in its glass
Shows the trained terrors, the well-practised partings,
The old woman standing at the cottage gate,
Her hand upon her grandson's shoulder. He,
A bundle of clouts creased as with tribulations,
Bristling with spikes and spits and bolts of steel,
Bound in with belts, the rifle's snub-nosed horn
Peering above his shoulder, looks across
From this new world to hers and tries to find
Some ordinary words that share her sorrow.
The stream flows on
And shows a blackened field, a burning wood,
A bridge that stops half-way, a hill split open
With scraps of houses clinging to its sides,
Stones, planks and tiles and chips of glass and china
Strewn on the slope as by a wrecking wave
Among the grass and wild-flowers. Darkness falls,
The stream flows through the city. In its mirror
Great oes and capitals and flourishes,
Pillars and towers and fans and gathered sheaves
Hold harvest-home and Judgment Day of fire.
The houses stir and pluck their roofs and walls

Apart as if in play and fling their stones
Against the sky to make a common arc
And fall again. The conflagrations raise
Their mountainous precipices. Living eyes
Glaze instantly in crystal change. The stream
Runs on into the day of time and Europe,
Past the familiar walls and friendly roads,
Now thronged with dumb migrations, gods and altars
That travel towards no destination. Then
The disciplined soldiers come to conquer nothing,
Narch upon emptiness and do not know
Why all is dead and life has hidden itself.
The enormous winding frontier walls fall down,
Leaving anonymous stone and vacant grass.
The stream flows on into what land, what peace,
Far past the other side of the burning world?

THEN

There were no men and women then at all,
But the flesh lying alone,
And angry shadows fighting on a wall
That now and then sent out a groan
Buried in lime and stone,
And sweated now and then like tortured wood
Big drops that looked yet did not look like blood.

And yet as each drop came a shadow faded
And left the wall.
There was a lull
Until another in its shadow arrayed it,
Came, fought and left a blood-mark on the wall;
And that was all; the blood was all.

If there had been women there they might have wept
For the poor blood, unowned, unwanted,
Blank as forgotten script.
The wall was haunted
By mute maternal presences whose sighing
Fluttered the fighting shadows and shook the wall
As if that fury of death itself were dying.

THE REFUGEES

A crack ran through our hearthstone long ago,
And from the fissure we watched gently grow
The tame domesticated danger,
Yet lived in comfort in our haunted rooms.
Till came the Stranger
And the great and the little dooms.

We saw the homeless waiting in the street
Year after year,
The always homeless,
Nationless and nameless,
To whose bare roof-trees never come
Peace and the house martin to make a home.
We did not fear
A wrong so dull and old,
So patiently told and patiently retold,
While we sat by the fire or in the window-seat.
Oh what these suffered in dumb animal patience,
That we now suffer,
While the world's brow grows darker and the world's hand
    rougher.
We bear the lot of nations,
Of times and races,

Because we watched the wrong
Last too long
With non-committal faces.
Until from Europe's sunset hill
We saw our houses falling
Wall after wall behind us.
What could blind us
To such self-evident ill
And all the sorrows from their caverns calling?

This is our punishment. We came
Here without blame, yet with blame,
Dark blame of others, but our blame also.
This stroke was bound to fall,
Though not to fall so.
A few years did not waste
The heaped up world. The central pillar fell
Moved by no living hand. The good fields sickened
By long infection. Oh this is the taste
Of evil done long since and always, quickened
No one knows how
While the red fruit hung ripe upon the bough
And fell at last and rotted where it fell.

For such things homelessness is ours
And shall be others'. Tenement roofs and towers
Will fall upon the kind and the unkind
Without election,
For deaf and blind
Is rejection bred by rejection
Breeding rejection,
And where no counsel is what will be will be.
We must shape here a new philosophy.

SCOTLAND 1941

We were a tribe, a family, a people.
Wallace and Bruce guard now a painted field,
And all may read the folio of our fable,
Peruse the sword, the sceptre and the shield.
A simple sky roofed in that rustic day,
The busy corn-fields and the haunted holms,
The green road winding up the ferny brae.
But Knox and Melville clapped their preaching palms
And bundled all the harvesters away,
Hoodicrow Peden in the blighted corn
Hacked with his rusty beak the starving haulms.
Out of that desolation we were born.

Courage beyond the point and obdurate pride
Made us a nation, robbed us of a nation.
Defiance absolute and myriad-eyed
That could not pluck the palm plucked our damnation.
We with such courage and the bitter wit
To fell the ancient oak of loyalty,
And strip the peopled hill and the altar bare,
And crush the poet with an iron text,
How could we read our souls and learn to be?
Here a dull drove of faces harsh and vexed,
We watch our cities burning in their pit,
To salve our souls grinding dull lucre out,
We, fanatics of the frustrate and the half,
Who once set Purgatory Hill in doubt.
Now smoke and dearth and money everywhere,
Mean heirlooms of each fainter generation,
And mummied housegods in their musty niches,
Burns and Scott, sham bards of a sham nation,
And spiritual defeat wrapped warm in riches,
No pride but pride of pelf. Long since the young

Fought in great bloody battles to carve out
This towering pulpit of the Golden Calf,
Montrose, Mackail, Argyle, perverse and brave,
Twisted the stream, unhooped the ancestral hill.
Never had Dee or Don or Yarrow or Till
Huddled such thriftless honour in a grave.

Such wasted bravery idle as a song,
Such hard-won ill might prove Time's verdict wrong,
And melt to pity the annalist's iron tongue.

THE LETTER

Tried friendship must go down perforce
Before the outward eating rage
And murderous heart of middle age,
Killing kind memory at its source,
If it were not for mortality,
The thought of that which levels all
And coldly pillows side by side
The tried friend and the too much tried.

Then think of that which will have made
Us and all else contemporary.
Look long enough and you will see
The dead fighting with the dead.
Now's the last hour for chivalry,
And we can still escape the shame
Of striking the unanswering head,
Before we are changed put off the blame.

But should this seem a niggardly
And ominous reconciliation,
Look again until you see,
Fixed in the body's final station,
The features of immortality.
Try to pursue this quarrel then.
You cannot. This is less than man
And more. That more is our salvation.
Now let us seize it. Now we can.

THE HUMAN FOLD

Here penned within the human fold
No longer now we shake the bars,
Although the ever-moving stars
Night after night in order rolled
Rebuke this stationary farce.
There's no alternative here but love,
So far as genuine love can be
Where there's no genuine liberty
To give or take, to lose or have,
And having rots with wrong, and loss
Itself has no security
Except in the well-managed grave,
And all we do is done to prove
Content and discontent both are gross.
Yet sometimes here we still can see
The dragon with his tears of gold,
The bat-browed sphinx
Shake loose her wings
That have no hold and fan no air,
All struck dead by her stare.
Hell shoots its avalanche at our feet,

In heaven the souls go up and down,
And we can see from this our seat
The heavenly and the hellish town,
The green cross growing in a wood
Close by old Eden's crumbling wall,
And God Himself in full manhood
Riding against the Fall.
All this; but here our sight is bound
By ten dull faces in a round,
Each with a made-to-measure glance
That is in misery till it's found.
Yet looking at each countenance
I read this burden in them all:
'I lean my cheek from eternity
For time to slap, for time to slap.
I gather my bones from the bottomless clay
To lay my head in the light's lap.'

By what long way, by what dark way,
From what unpredetermined place,
Did we creep severally to this hole
And bring no memory and no grace
To furnish evidence of the soul,
Though come of an ancient race?
All gone, where now we cannot say,
Altar and shrine and boundary stone,
And of the legends of our day
This one remains alone:
'They loved and might have loved for ever,
But public trouble and private care
Faith and hope and love can sever
And strip the bed and the altar bare'.
Forward our towering shadows fall
Upon the naked nicheless wall,
And all we see is that shadow-dance.

Yet looking at each countenance
I read this burden in them all:
'I lean my cheek from eternity
For time to slap, for time to slap.
I gather my bones from the bottomless clay
To lay my head in the light's lap'.

THE NARROW PLACE

How all the roads creep in.
This place has grown so narrow,
You could not swing a javelin,
And if you shot an arrow,
It would skim this meagre mountain wall
And in some other country
Like a lost meteor fall.
When first this company
Took root here no one knows,
For nothing comes and goes
But the bleak mountain wind,
That so our blood has thinned
And sharpened so our faces—
Unanswerably grave
As long-forsaken places—
They have lost all look of hate or love
And keep but what they have.
The cloud has drawn so close,
This small much-trodden mound
Must, must be very high
And no road goes by.
The parsimonious ground
That at its best will bear
A few thin blades as fine as hair

Can anywhere be found,
Yet is so proud and niggardly
And envious, it will trust
Only one little wild half-leafless tree
To straggle from the dust.

Yet under it we sometimes feel such ease
As if it were ten thousand trees
And for its foliage had
Robbed half the world of shade.
All the woods in grief
Bowed down by leaf and bird and leaf
From all their branches could not weep
A sleep such as that sleep.

Sleep underneath the tree.
It is your murdering eyes that make
The sterile hill, the standing lake,
And the leaf-breaking wind.
Then shut your eyes and see,
Sleep on and do not wake
Till there is movement in the lake,
And the club-headed water-serpents break
In emerald lightnings through the slime,
Making a mark on Time.

THE RECURRENCE

All things return, Nietzsche said,
The ancient wheel revolves again,
Rise, take up your numbered fate;
The cradle and the bridal bed,
Life and the coffin wait.

All has been that ever can be,
And this sole eternity
Cannot cancel, cannot add
One to your delights or tears,
Or a million million years
Tear the nightmare from the mad.

Have no fear then. You will miss
Achievement by the self-same inch,
When the great occasion comes
And they watch you, you will flinch,
Lose the moment, be for bliss
A footlength short. All done before.
Love's agonies, victory's drums
Cannot huddle the Cross away
Planted on its future hill.
The secret on the appointed day
Will be made known, the ship once more
Hit upon the waiting rock
Or come safely to the shore,
Careless under the deadly tree
The victim drowse, the urgent warning
Come too late, the dagger strike,
Strike and strike through eternity,
And worlds hence the prison clock
Will toll on execution morning,
What is ill be always ill,
Wretches die behind a dike,
And the happy be happy still.

But the heart makes reply:
This is only what the eye
From its tower on the turning field
Sees and sees and cannot tell why,
Quarterings on the turning shield,

The great non-stop heraldic show.
And the heart and the mind know,
What has been can never return,
What is not will surely be
In the changed unchanging reign,
Else the Actor on the Tree
Would loll at ease, miming pain,
And counterfeit mortality.

THE GOOD MAN IN HELL

If a good man were ever housed in Hell
    By needful error of the qualities,
Perhaps to prove the rule or shame the devil,
    Or speak the truth only a stranger sees,

Would he, surrendering to obvious hate,
    Fill half eternity with cries and tears,
Or watch beside Hell's little wicket gate
    In patience for the first ten thousand years,

Feeling the curse climb slowly to his throat
    That, uttered, dooms him to rescindless ill,
Forcing his praying tongue to run by rote,
    Eternity entire before him still?

Would he at last, grown faithful in his station,
    Kindle a little hope in hopeless Hell,
And sow among the damned doubts of damnation,
    Since here someone could live and could live well?

One doubt of evil would bring down such a grace,
    Open such a gate, all Eden would enter in,
Hell be a place like any other place,
    And love and hate and life and death begin.

THE WHEEL

How can I turn this wheel that turns my life,
Create another hand to move this hand
Not moved by me, who am not the mover,
Nor, though I love and hate, the lover,
The hater? Loves and hates are thrust
Upon me by the acrimonious dead,
The buried thesis, long since rusted knife,
Revengeful dust.
A stony or obstreperous head,
Though slain so squarely, can usurp my will
As I walk above it on the sunny hill.

Then how do I stand?
How can I here remake what there made me
And makes and remakes me still?
Set a new mark? Circumvent history?
Nothing can come of history but history,
The stationary storm that cannot bate
Its neutral violence,
The transitory solution that cannot wait,
The indecisive victory
That is like loss read backwards and cannot bring
Relief to you and me,
The jangling
Of all the voices of plant and beast and man
That have not made a harmony
Since first the great controversy began,
And cannot sink to silence
Unless a grace
Come of itself to wrap our souls in peace
Between the turning leaves of history and make
Ourselves ourselves, winnow the grudging grain,
And take
From that which made us that which will make us again.

THE FACE

See me with all the terrors on my roads,
The crusted shipwrecks rotting in my seas,
And the untroubled oval of my face
That alters idly with the moonlike modes
And is unfathomably framed to please
And deck the angular bone with passing grace.

I should have worn a terror-mask, should be
A sight to frighten hope and faith away,
Half charnel field, half battle and rutting ground.
Instead I am a smiling summer sea
That sleeps while underneath from bound to bound
The sun- and star-shaped killers gorge and play.

THE LAW

O you my Law
Which I serve not,
O you my Good
Which I prize not,
O you my Truth
Which I seek not:

Where grace is beyond desert
Thanks must be thanklessness;
Where duty is past performance
Disservice is only service;
Where truth is unsearchable
All seeking is straying.

If I could know ingratitude's
Bounds I should know gratitude;
And disservice done
Would show me the law of service;
And the wanderer at last
Learns his long error.

If I could hold complete
The reverse side of the pattern,
The wrong side of Heaven,
O then I should know in not knowing
My truth in my error.

THE CITY

Day after day we kept the dusty road,
    And nearer came small-towered Jerusalem,
Nearer and nearer. Lightened of the goad,
    Our beasts went on as if the air wafted them.

We saw the other troops with music move
    Between the mountain meadows, far and clear,
Onwards towards the city, and above
    The ridge the fresh young firmament looked near.

All stood so silent in the silent air,
    The little houses set on every hill,
A tree before each house. The people were
    Tranquil, not sad nor glad. How they could till

Their simple fields, here, almost at the end,
    Perplexed us. We were filled with dumb surprise
At wells and mills, and could not understand
    This was an order natural and wise.

107

We looked away. Yet some of us declared:
    'Let us stay here. We ask no more than this,'
Though we were now so close, we who had dared
    Half the world's spite to hit the mark of bliss.

So we went on to the end. But there we found
    A dead land pitted with blind whirling places,
And crowds of angry men who held their ground
    With blank blue eyes and raging rubicund faces.

We drew our swords and in our minds we saw
    The streets of the holy city running with blood,
And centuries of fear and power and awe,
    And all our children in the deadly wood.

THE GROVE

There was no road at all to that high place
But through the smothering grove,
Where as we went the shadows wove
Adulterous shapes of animal hate and love.
The idol-crowded nightmare Space,
Wood beyond wood, tree behind tree,
And every tree an empty face
Gashed by the casual lightning mark
The first great Luciferian animal
Scored on leaf and bark.
This was, we knew, the heraldic ground,
And therefore now we heard our footsteps fall
With the true legendary sound,
Like secret trampling behind a wall,
As if they were saying: To be: to be.

And oh the silence, the drugged thicket dozing
Deep in its dream of fear,
The ring closing
And coming near,
The well-bred self-sufficient animals
With clean rank pelts and proud and fetid breath,
Screaming their arrogant calls,
Their moonstone eyes set straight at life and death.
Did we see or dream it? And the jungle cities—
For there were cities there and civilizations
Deep in the forest; powers and dominations
Like shapes begotten by dreaming animals,
Proud animal dreams uplifted high,
Booted and saddled on the animal's back
And staring with the arrogant animal's eye:
The golden dukes, the silver earls, and gleaming black
The curvetting knights sitting their curvetting steeds,
The sweet silk-tunicked eunuchs singing ditties,
Swaying like wandering weeds,
The scarlet cardinals,
And lions high in the air on the banner's field,
Crowns, sceptres, spears and stars and moons of blood,
And sylvan wars in bronze within the shield,
All quartered in the wide world's wood,
The smothering grove where there was place for pities.

We trod the maze like horses in a mill,
And then passed through it
As in a dream of the will.
How could it be? There was the stifling grove,
Yet here was light; what wonder led us to it?
How could the blind path go
To climb the crag and top the towering hill,
And all that splendour spread? We know
There was no road except the smothering grove.

THE GATE

We sat, two children, warm against the wall
Outside the towering stronghold of our fathers
That frowned its stern security down upon us.
We could not enter there. That fortress life,
Our safe protection, was too gross and strong
For our unpractised palates. Yet our guardians
Cherished our innocence with gentle hands,
(They, who had long since lost their innocence,)
And in grave play put on a childish mask
Over their tell-tale faces, as in shame
For the rich food that plumped their lusty bodies
And made them strange as gods. We sat that day
With that great parapet behind us, safe
As every day, yet outcast, safe and outcast
As castaways thrown upon an empty shore.
Before us lay the well-worn scene, a hillock
So small and smooth and green, it seemed intended
For us alone and childhood, a still pond
That opened upon no sight a quiet eye,
A little stream that tinkled down the slope.
But suddenly all seemed old
And dull and shrunken, shut within itself
In a sullen dream. We were outside, alone.
And then behind us the huge gate swung open.

THE LITTLE GENERAL

Early in spring the little General came
    Across the sound, bringing the island death,
And suddenly a place without a name,
    And like the pious ritual of a faith,

Hunter and quarry in the boundless trap,
  The white smoke curling from the silver gun,
The feather curling in the hunter's cap,
  And clouds of feathers floating in the sun,

While down the birds came in a deafening shower,
  Wing-hurricane, and the cattle fled in fear.
Up on the hill a remnant of a tower
  Had watched that single scene for many a year,

Weaving a wordless tale where all were gathered
  (Hunter and quarry and watcher and fabulous field),
A sylvan war half human and half feathered,
  Perennial emblem painted on the shield

Held up to cow a never-conquered land
Fast in the little General's fragile hand.

THE PRIZE

Did we come here, drawn by some fatal thing,
Fly from eternity's immaculate bow
Straight to the heart of time's great turning ring,
That we might win the prize that took us so?
Was it some ordinary sight, a flower,
The white wave falling, falling upon the shore,
The blue of the sky, the grasses' waving green?

Or was it one sole thing, a certain door
Set in a wall, a half-conjectured scene
Of men and women moving as in a play,
A turn in the winding road, a distant tower,

A corner of a field, a single place
Apart, a single house, a single tree,
A look upon one half-averted face
That has been once, or is, or is to be?

We hurried here for some such thing and now
Wander the countless roads to seek our prize,
That far within the maze serenely lies,
While all around each trivial shape exclaims:
'Here is your jewel; this is your longed for day',
And we forget, lost in the countless names.

THE SHADES

The bodiless spirits waiting chill
In the ports of black Nonentity
For passage to the living land,
Without eyes strive to see,
Without ears strain to hear,
Stretch an unincarnate hand
In greeting to the hollow hill
Above the insubstantial sea,
The billow curving on the sand,
The bird sitting on the tree;
And in love and in fear
Ensnare the smile, condense the tear,
Rehearse the play of evil and good,
The comedy and the tragedy.
Until the summoned ghosts appear
In patterned march around the hill
Against the hoofed and horned wood.

THE RING

Long since we were a family, a people,
The legends say; an old kind-hearted king
Was our foster father, and our life a fable.

Nature in wrath broke through the grassy ring
Where all our gathered treasures lay in sleep—
Many a rich and many a childish thing.

She filled with hoofs and horns the quiet keep.
Her herds beat down the turf and nosed the shrine
In bestial wonder, bull and adder and ape,

Lion and fox, all dressed by fancy fine
In human flesh and armed with arrows and spears;
But on the brow of each a secret sign

That haughtily put aside the sorrowful years
Or struck them down in stationary rage;
Yet they had tears that were not like our tears,

And new, all new, for Nature knows no age.
Fatherless, sonless, homeless haunters, they
Had never known the vow and the pilgrimage,

Poured from one fount into the faithless day.
We are their sons, but long ago we heard
Our fathers or our fathers' fathers say

Out of their dream the long-forgotten word
That rounded again the ring where sleeping lay
Our treasures, still unrusted and unmarred.

THE RETURN OF ODYSSEUS

The doors flapped open in Odysseus' house,
The lolling latches gave to every hand,
Let traitor, babbler, tout and bargainer in.
The rooms and passages resounded
With ease and chaos of a public market,
The walls mere walls to lean on as you talked,
Spat on the floor, surveyed some newcomer
With an absent eye. There you could be yourself.
Dust in the nooks, weeds nodding in the yard,
The thick walls crumbling. Even the cattle came
About the doors with mild familiar stare
As if this were their place.
All round the island stretched the clean blue sea.

Sole at the house's heart Penelope
Sat at her chosen task, endless undoing
Of endless doing, endless weaving, unweaving,
In the clean chamber. Still her loom ran empty
Day after day. She thought: 'Here I do nothing
Or less than nothing, making an emptiness
Amid disorder, weaving, unweaving the lie
The day demands. Odysseus, this is duty,
To do and undo, to keep a vacant gate
Where order and right and hope and peace can enter.
Oh will you ever return? Or are you dead,
And this wrought emptiness my ultimate emptiness?'

She wove and unwove and wove and did not know
That even then Odysseus on the long
And winding road of the world was on his way.

ROBERT THE BRUCE

To Douglas in Dying:

'My life is done, yet all remains,
  The breath has gone, the image not,
The furious shapes once forged in heat
  Live on though now no longer hot.

'Steadily the shining swords
  In order rise, in order fall,
In order on the beaten field
  The faithful trumpets call.

'The women weeping for the dead
  Are not sad now but dutiful,
The dead men stiffening in their place
  Proclaim the ancient rule.

'Great Wallace's body hewn in four,
  So altered, stays as it must be.
O Douglas do not leave me now,
  For past your head I see

'My dagger sheathed in Comyn's heart
  And nothing there to praise or blame,
Nothing but order which must be
  Itself and still the same.

'But that Christ hung upon the Cross,
  Comyn would rot until time's end
And bury my sin in boundless dust,
  For there is no amend

'In order; yet in order run
   All things by unreturning ways.
If Christ live not, nothing is there
   For sorrow or for praise.'

So the King spoke to Douglas once
   A little while before his death,
Having outfaced three English kings
   And kept a people's faith.

THE TROPHY

The wise king dowered with blessings on his throne,
The rebel raising the flag in the market place,
Haunt me like figures on an ancient stone
The ponderous light of history beats upon,
Or the enigma of a single face
Handed unguessed, unread from father to son,
As if it dreamed within itself alone.

Regent and rebel clash in horror and blood
Here on the blindfold battlefield. But there,
Motionless in the grove of evil and good
They grow together and their roots are twined
In deep confederacy far from the air,
Sharing the secret trophy each with other;
And king and rebel are like brother and brother,
Or father and son, co-princes of one mind,
Irreconcilables, their treaty signed.

THE ANNUNCIATION

Now in this iron reign
I sing the liberty
Where each asks from each
What each most wants to give
And each awakes in each
What else would never be,
Summoning so the rare
Spirit to breathe and live.

Then let us empty out
Our hearts until we find
The last least trifling toy,
Since now all turns to gold,
And everything we have
Is wealth of heart and mind,
That squandered thus in turn
Grows with us manifold.

Giving, I'd give you next
Some more than mortal grace,
But that you deifying
Myself I might deify,
Forgetting love was born
Here in a time and place,
And robbing by such praise
This life we magnify.

Whether the soul at first
This pilgrimage began,
Or the shy body leading
Conducted soul to soul
Who knows? This is the most
That soul and body can,
To make us each for each
And in our spirit whole.

THE CONFIRMATION

Yes, yours, my love, is the right human face.
I in my mind had waited for this long,
Seeing the false and searching for the true,
Then found you as a traveller finds a place
Of welcome suddenly amid the wrong
Valleys and rocks and twisting roads. But you,
What shall I call you? A fountain in a waste,
A well of water in a country dry,
Or anything that's honest and good, an eye
That makes the whole world bright. Your open heart,
Simple with giving, gives the primal deed,
The first good world, the blossom, the blowing seed,
The hearth, the steadfast land, the wandering sea,
Not beautiful or rare in every part,
But like yourself, as they were meant to be.

THE COMMEMORATION

I wish I could proclaim
My faith enshrined in you
And spread among a few
Our high but hidden fame,
That we new life have spun
Past all that's thought and done,
And someone or no one
Might tell both did the same.

Material things will pass
And we have seen the flower
And the slow falling tower
Lie gently in the grass,

But meantime we have stored
Riches past bed and board
And nursed another hoard
Than callow lad and lass.

Invisible virtue now
Expands upon the air
Although no fruit appear
Nor weight bend down the bough,
And harvests truly grown
For someone or no one
Are stored and safely won
In hollow heart and brow.

How can one thing remain
Except the invisible,
The echo of a bell
Long rusted in the rain?
This strand we weave into
Our monologue of two,
And time cannot undo
That strong and subtle chain.

THE OLD GODS

Old gods and goddesses who have lived so long
Through time and never found eternity,
Fettered by wasting wood and hollowing hill,

You should have fled our ever-dying song.
The mound, the well, and the green trysting tree,
They are forgotten, yet you linger still.

Goddess of caverned breast and channelled brow
And cheeks slow hollowed by millenial tears,
Forests of autumns fading in your eyes,

Eternity marvels at your counted years
And kingdoms lost in time, and wonders how
There could be thoughts so bountiful and wise

As yours beneath the ever-breaking bough,
And vast compassion curving like the skies.

THE BIRD

Adventurous bird walking upon the air,
Like a schoolboy running and loitering, leaping and springing,
Pensively pausing, suddenly changing your mind
To turn at ease on the heel of a wing-tip. Where
In all the crystalline world was there to find
For your so delicate walking and airy winging
A floor so perfect, so firm and so fair,
And where a ceiling and walls so sweetly ringing,
Whenever you sing, to your clear singing?

The wide-winged soul itself can ask no more
Than such a pure, resilient and endless floor
For its strong-pinioned plunging and soaring and upward and
   upward springing.

THE GUESS

We buried them beneath the deep green hill—
A little Ark full, women, men and cattle,
Children and household pets, engrossed by war.
And then one morning they were back again
And held as once before their little reign.
All joys and sorrows but the last were there:
That day erased: no pit or mound of battle.
They lay as by some happy chance reborn
An hour or two before the birth of ill,
And ere ill came they'd be away again.
Quick leave and brief reward, so lightly worn.

I watched them move between sleep and awake.
It was a dream and could not be fulfilled,
For all these ghosts were blessed. Yet there seemed
Nothing more natural than blessedness,
Nor any life as true as this I dreamed,
So that I did not feel that I had willed
These forms, but that a long forgotten guess
Had shown, past chaos, the natural shape we take.

THE SWIMMER'S DEATH

He lay outstretched upon the sunny wave,
That turned and broke into eternity.
The light showed nothing but a glassy grave
Among the trackless tumuli of the sea.
Then over his buried brow and eyes and lips
From every side flocked in the homing ships.

THE QUESTION

Will you, sometime, who have sought so long and seek
Still in the slowly darkening hunting ground,
Catch sight some ordinary month or week
Of that strange quarry you scarcely thought you sought—
Yourself, the gatherer gathered, the finder found,
The buyer, who would buy all, in bounty bought—
And perch in pride on the princely hand, at home,
And there, the long hunt over, rest and roam?

THE DAY

If, in the mind of God or book of fate,
This day that's all to live lies lived and done,
And there already like Griseldas wait
My apprentice thoughts and actions, still untried;
If, where I travel, some thing or some one
Has gone before me sounding through the wide
Immensity of nothingness to make
A region and a road where road was none,
Nor shape, nor shaping hand; if for my sake
The elected joy grows there and the chosen pain
In the field of good and ill, in surety sown:
Oh give me clarity and love that now
The way I walk may truly trace again
The in eternity written and hidden way;
Make pure my heart and will, and me allow
The acceptance and revolt, the yea and nay,
The denial and the blessing that are my own.

The Voyage

1946

THE RETURN OF THE GREEKS

The veteran Greeks came home
Sleepwandering from the war.
We saw the galleys come
Blundering over the bar.
Each soldier with his scar
In rags and tatters came home.

Reading the wall of Troy
Ten years without a change
Was such intense employ
(Just out of the arrows' range),
All the world was strange
After ten years of Troy.

Their eyes knew every stone
In the huge heartbreaking wall
Year after year grown
Till there was nothing at all
But an alley steep and small,
Tramped earth and towering stone.

Now even the hills seemed low
In the boundless sea and land,
Weakened by distance so.
How could they understand
Space empty on every hand
And the hillocks squat and low?

And when they arrived at last
They found a childish scene
Embosomed in the past,
And the war lying between—
A child's preoccupied scene
When they came home at last.

But everything trite and strange,
The peace, the parcelled ground,
The vinerows—never a change!
The past and the present bound
In one oblivious round
Past thinking trite and strange.

But for their grey-haired wives
And their sons grown shy and tall
They would have given their lives
To raise the battered wall
Again, if this was all
In spite of their sons and wives.

Penelope in her tower
Looked down upon the show
And saw within an hour
Each man to his wife go,
Hesitant, sure and slow:
She, alone in her tower.

THE ESCAPE

Escaping from the enemy's hand
    Into the enemy's vast domain,
I sought by many a devious path,
    Having got in, to get out again.

The endless trap lay everywhere,
    And all the roads ran in a maze
Hither and thither, like a web
    To catch the careless days.

The great farmhouses sunk in time
    Rose up out of another land;
Here only the empty harvest-home
    Where Caliban waved his wand.

There was no promise in the bud,
    No comfort in the blossoming tree,
The waving yellow harvests were
    Worse than sterility.

Yet all seemed true. The family group
    Still gathered round the dying hearth,
The old men droned the ancient saws,
    And the young mother still gave birth.

But this I saw there. In the church
    In rows the stabled horses stood,
And the cottar's threshold stone
    Was mired with earth and blood.

And when I reached the line between
    The Occupied and Unoccupied,
It was as hard as death to cross,
    Yet no change on the other side.

All false, all one. The enemy
    These days was scarcely visible;
Only his work was everywhere,
    Ill work contrived so well

That he could smile and turn his back,
    Let brute indifference overawe
The longing flesh and leaping heart
    And grind to dust the ancient law.

A land of bright delusion where
    Shape scarce disturbed the emptiness
Yet troubled the sight that strove to make
    Of every shape a shape the less.

There the perpetual question ran,
    What is escape? and What is flight?
Like dialogue in a dismal dream
    Where right is wrong and wrong is right.

But at the very frontier line,
    Beyond the region of desire,
There runs a wall of towering flame:
    The battle is there of blood and fire.

I must pass through that fiery wall,
    Emerge into the battle place,
And there at last, lifting my eyes,
    I'll see the enemy's face.

THE CASTLE

All through that summer at ease we lay,
And daily from the turret wall
We watched the mowers in the hay
And the enemy half a mile away.
They seemed no threat to us at all.

For what, we thought, had we to fear
With our arms and provender, load on load,
Our towering battlements, tier on tier,
And friendly allies drawing near
On every leafy summer road.

Our gates were strong, our walls were thick,
So smooth and high, no man could win
A foothold there, no clever trick
Could take us, have us dead or quick.
Only a bird could have got in.

What could they offer us for bait?
Our captain was brave and we were true . . .
There was a little private gate,
A little wicked wicket gate.
The wizened warder let them through.

Oh then our maze of tunnelled stone
Grew thin and treacherous as air.
The cause was lost without a groan,
The famous citadel overthrown,
And all its secret galleries bare.

How can this shameful tale be told?
I will maintain until my death
We could do nothing, being sold;
Our only enemy was gold,
And we had no arms to fight it with.

MOSES

He left us there, went up to Pisgah hill,
And saw the holiday land, the sabbath land,
The mild prophetic beasts, millennial herds,
The sacred lintel, over-arching tree,
The vineyards glittering on the southern slopes,
And in the midst the shining vein of water,
The river turning, turning towards its home.
Promised to us. The dream rose in his nostrils
With homely smell of wine and corn and cattle,

Byre, barn and stall, sweat-sanctified smell of peace.
He saw the tribes arrayed beside the river,
White robes and sabbath stillness, still light falling
On dark heads whitened by the desert wave,
The Sabbath of Sabbaths come and Canaan their home.
All this he saw in dreaming. But we who dream
Such common dreams and see so little saw
The battle for the land, the massacres,
The vineyards drenched in aboriginal blood,
The settlement, unsatisfactory order,
The petty wars and neighbouring jealousies
And local troubles. But we did not see,
We did not see and Moses did not see,
The great disaster, exile, diaspora,
The holy bread of the land crumbled and broken
In Babylon, Caesarea, Alexandria
As on a splendid dish, or gnawed as offal.
Nor did we see, beyond, the ghetto rising,
Toledo, Cracow, Vienna, Budapesth,
Nor, had we seen, would we have known our people
In the wild disguises of fantastic time,
Packed in dense cities, wandering countless roads,
And not a road in the world to lead them home.
How could we have seen such things? How could we have seen
That plot of ground pledged by the God of Moses
Trampled by sequent tribes, seized and forgotten
As a child seizes and forgets a toy,
Strange languages, strange gods and customs borne
Over it and away with the light migrations,
Stirring each century ancestral dust.
All this was settled while we stood by Jordan
That first great day, could not be otherwise.
Moses saw that day only; we did not see it;
But now it stands becalmed in time for ever:
White robes and sabbath peace, the snow-white emblem.

SAPPHO

Sappho, Sappho's pitiless murderess,
Strides in judgment through the end of night
To circumvent the round blue trap of day
(That soon will lock its jail of miseries),
Drives her victim to the penal rock,
Angry, abrupt, broken-off edge of time.
Pursuer and pursued
Tied each to each by such a sullen knot
No arrowy thought of immaterial god
Can slip between and ease the torment crying:
'All my life cries out against all my life,
My love against all my love. I'll carry Phaon
Until I drop or leap the final crag
Where all is left behind, things and their names.
For if a single name should follow there
I must reiterate this death and leap
Precipice after precipice of death
Till name of wood and hill and night and day
And all that summons Phaon is stripped off.'

Now the dumb hulks of being rise around her:
Beast, rock and tree, illegible figures, stare
At her in destitution as on the day
Before the first day broke, when all was nameless,
Nameless earth, water, firmament, and nameless
Woman and man. Till on the utmost edge
She leans above the unanswering shapes of life,
Cries once and leaps, and battered on the stones,
Batters love, Phaon and all the misery out.

THE COVENANT

The covenant of god and animal,
The frieze of fabulous creatures winged and crowned,
And in the midst the woman and the man—

Lost long ago in fields beyond the Fall—
Keep faith in sleep-walled night and there are found
On our long journey back where we began.

Then the heraldic crest of nature lost
Shines out again until the weariless wave
Roofs with its sliding horror all that realm.

What jealousy, what rage could overwhelm
The golden lion and lamb and vault a grave
For innocence, innocence past defence or cost?

THOUGHT AND IMAGE

Past time and space the shaping Thought
   Was born in freedom and in play;
The Image then on earth was wrought
   Of water and of clay.

And when the embodied Soul would know
   Itself and be to itself revealed,
For its instruction it must go
   To the beast that roams the field.

Thenceforth the Soul grew intimate
   With beast and herb and stone, and passed
Into the elements to mate
   With the dull earth at last.

It's said that to reverse its doom
    And save the entangled Soul, to earth
God came and entered in the womb
    And passed through the gate of birth;

Was born a Child in body bound
    Among the cattle in a byre.
The clamorous world was all around,
    Beast, insect, plant, earth, water, fire.

On bread and wine his flesh grew tall,
    The round sun helped him on his way,
Wood, iron, herb and animal
    His friends were till the testing day.

Then braced by iron and by wood,
    Engrafted on a tree he died,
And little dogs lapped up the blood
    That spurted from his broken side.

The great bull gored him with his horns,
    And stinging flies were everywhere,
The sun beat on him, clinging thorns
    Writhed in and out among his hair.

His body next was locked in stone,
    By steel preserved in sterile trust,
And with the earth was left alone,
    And, dust, lay with the dust.

There all at last with all was done,
    The great knot loosened, flesh unmade
Beyond the kingdom of the sun,
    In the invincible shade.

All that had waited for his birth
  Were round him then in dusty night,
The creatures of the swarming earth,
  The souls and angels in the height.

TWICE-DONE, ONCE-DONE

Nothing yet was ever done
  Till it was done again,
And no man was ever one
  Except through dead men.

I could neither rise nor fall
  But that Adam fell.
Had he fallen once for all
  There'd be nothing to tell.

Unless in me my fathers live
  I can never show
I am myself—ignorant if
  I'm a ghost or no.

Father Adam and Mother Eve,
  Make this pact with me:
Teach me, teach me to believe,
  For to believe's to be.

Many a woman since Eve was made
  Has seen the world is young,
Many and many a time obeyed
  The legend-making tongue.

Abolish the ancient custom—who
    Would mark Eve on her shelf?
Even a story to be true
    Must repeat itself.

Yet we the latest born are still
    The first ones and the last,
And in our little measures fill
    The oceanic past.

For first and last is every way,
    And first and last each soul,
And first and last the passing day,
    And first and last the goal.

THE VOYAGE

(For Eric Linklater)

That sea was greater than we knew.
Week after week the empty round
Went with us; the Unchanging grew,
And we were headed for that bound.

How we came there we could not tell.
Seven storms had piled us in that peace,
Put us in check and barred us well
With seven walls of seven seas.

As one may vanish in a day
In some untravelled fold of space
And there pursue his patient way
Yet never come to any place

Though following still by star and sun,
For every chart is rased and furled,
And he out of this world has run
And wanders now another world,

So we by line and compass steered
And conned the book of sun and star,
Yet where it should no sign appeared
To tell us, You are there or there,

Familiar landfall, slender mast:
We on the ocean were alone.
The busy lanes where fleets had passed
Showed us no sail except our own.

Still south we steered day after day
And only water lay around
As if the land had stolen away
Or sprawled upon the ocean ground.

The sun by day, the stars by night
Had only us to look upon,
Bent on us their collected light,
And followed on as we went on.

Sometimes in utter wonder lost
That loneliness like this could be
We stood and stared until almost
We saw no longer sky or sea,

But only the frame of time and space,
An empty floor, a vacant wall,
And on that blank no line to trace
Movement, if we moved at all.

What thoughts came then! Sometimes it seemed
We long had passed the living by
On other seas and only dreamed
This sea, this journey and this sky,

Or traced a ghostly parallel
That limned the land but could not merge,
And haven and home and harbour bell
Were just behind the horizon verge,

Or the world itself had ended so
Without a cry, and we should sail
To and fro, to and fro,
Long past the lightning and the gale.

O then what crowding fantasies
Poured in from empty sea and sky!
At night we heard the whispering quays,
Line after line, slide softly by.

Delusions in the silent noon;
Fields in the hollows of the waves;
Or spread beneath the yellow moon,
A land of harvests and of graves.

The soft sea-sounds beguiled our ear.
We thought we walked by mountain rills
Or listened half a night to hear
The spring wind hunting on the hills.

And faces, faces, faces came
Across the salt sea–desert air,
And rooms in which a candle flame
Made everything renowned and rare.

The words we knew like our right hand,
Mountain and valley, meadow and grove,
Composed a legendary land
Rich with the broken tombs of love.

Delusion or truth? We were content
Thenceforth to sail the harmless seas
Safe past the Fate and the Accident,
And called a blessing on that peace.

And blessing, we ourselves were blest,
Lauded the loss that brought our gain,
Sang the tumultuous world to rest,
And wishless called it back again.

For loss was then our only joy,
Privation of all, fulfilled desire,
The world our treasure and our toy
In destitution clean as fire.

Our days were then—I cannot tell
How we were then fulfilled and crowned
With life as in a parable,
And sweetly as gods together bound.

Delusion and dream! Our captain knew
Compass and clock had never yet
Failed him; the sun and stars were true.
The mark was there that we should hit.

And it rose up, a sullen stain
Flawing the crystal firmament.
A wound! We felt the familiar pain
And knew the place to which we were sent.

THE FATHERS

Our fathers all were poor,
Poorer our fathers' fathers;
Beyond, we dare not look.
We, the sons, keep store
Of tarnished gold that gathers
Around us from the night,
Record it in this book
That, when the line is drawn,
Credit and creditor gone,
Column and figure flown,
Will open into light.

Archaic fevers shake
Our healthy flesh and blood
Plumped in the passing day
And fed with pleasant food.
The fathers' anger and ache
Will not, will not away
And leave the living alone,
But on our careless brows
Faintly their furrows engrave
Like veinings in a stone,
Breathe in the sunny house
Nightmare of blackened bone,
Cellar and choking cave.

Panics and furies fly
Through our unhurried veins,
Heavenly lights and rains
Purify heart and eye,
Past agonies purify
And lay the sullen dust.
The angers will not away.

We hold our fathers' trust,
Wrong, riches, sorrow and all
Until they topple and fall,
And fallen let in the day.

THE THREE MIRRORS

I looked in the first glass
And saw the fenceless field
And like broken stones in grass
The sad towns glint and shine.
The slowly twisting vine
Scribbled with wrath the stone,
The mountain summits were sealed
In incomprehensible wrath.
The hunting roads ran on
To round the flying hill
And bring the quarry home.
But the obstinate roots ran wrong,
The lumbering fate fell wrong,
The walls were askew with ill,
Askew went every path,
The dead lay askew in the tomb.

I looked in the second glass
And saw through the twisted scroll
In virtue undefiled
And new in eternity
Father and mother and child,
The house with its single tree,
Bed and board and cross,
And the dead asleep in the knoll.

But the little blade and leaf
By an angry law were bent
To shapes of terror and grief,
By a law the field was rent,
The crack ran over the floor,
The child at peace in his play
Changed as he passed through a door,
Changed were the house and the tree,
Changed the dead in the knoll,
For locked in love and grief
Good with evil lay.

If I looked in the third glass
I should see evil and good
Standing side by side
In the ever standing wood,
The wise king safe on his throne,
The rebel raising the rout,
And each so deeply grown
Into his own place
He'd be past desire or doubt.
If I could look I should see
The world's house open wide,
The million million rooms
And the quick god everywhere
Glowing at work and at rest,
Tranquillity in the air,
Peace of the humming looms
Weaving from east to west,
And you and myself there.

THE RIDER VICTORY

The rider Victory reins his horse
Midway across the empty bridge
As if head-tall he had met a wall.
Yet there was nothing there at all,
No bodiless barrier, ghostly ridge
To check the charger in his course
So suddenly, you'd think he'd fall.

Suspended, horse and rider stare
Leaping on air and legendary.
In front the waiting kingdom lies,
The bridge and all the roads are free;
But halted in implacable air
Rider and horse with stony eyes
Uprear their motionless statuary.

THE WINDOW

Within the great wall's perfect round
Bird, beast and child serenely grew
In endless change on changeless ground
That in a single pattern bound
The old perfection and the new.

There was a tower set in the wall
And a great window in the tower,
And if one looked, beyond recall
The twisting glass kept him in thrall
With changing marvels hour by hour.
And there one day we looked and saw
Marsh, mere and mount in anger shaken,

The world's great side, the giant flaw,
And watched the stately forests fall,
The white ships sinking in the sea,
The tower run toppling in the field,
The last left stronghold sacked and taken,
And earth and heaven in jeopardy.
Then turning towards you I beheld
The wrinkle writhe across your brow,
And felt time's cap clapped on my head,
And all within the enclosure now,
Light leaf and smiling flower, was false,
The great wall breached, the garden dead.

Across the towering window fled
Disasters, victories, festivals.

THE HOUSE

The young and the lusty loll in bed
And the bent and the aged lay the fire
And sweep the floor and cook the food.
'No reason or rule is in this house,'

Sighed the little old woman, shaking her head,
'Where the young and the rich have their desire,
And all the reward of the poor and the good
Is to prop the walls of this thankless house.

'Yes,' she muttered '*they*'ve all they want,
But we have nothing but knowledge to chew,
Only that, and necessity.
These two maintain this niggardly house.

143

'For the young and the rich are ignorant
And never guess what they've yet to rue—
The lenten days when they will be
Servants like us of this tyrannous house.'

THE MYTH

My childhood all a myth
Enacted in a distant isle;
Time with his hourglass and his scythe
Stood dreaming on the dial,
And did not move the whole day long
That immobility might save
Continually the dying song,
The flower, the falling wave.
And at each corner of the wood
In which I played the ancient play,
Guarding the traditional day
The faithful watchers stood.

My youth a tragi-comedy,
Ridiculous war of dreams and shames
Waged for a Pyrrhic victory
Of reveries and names,
Which in slow-motion rout were hurled
Before sure-footed flesh and blood
That of its hunger built a world,
Advancing rood by rood.
And there in practical clay compressed
The reverie played its useful part,
Fashioning a diurnal mart
Of radiant east and west.

So manhood went. Now past the prime
I see this life contrived to stay
With all its works of labouring time
By time beguiled away.
Consolidated flesh and bone
And its designs grow halt and lame;
Unshakeable arise alone
The reverie and the name.
And at each border of the land,
Like monuments a deluge leaves,
Guarding the invisible sheaves
The risen watchers stand.

ON SEEING TWO LOVERS IN THE STREET

You do not know
What is done with you,
Do not fear
What's done or undone:
You are not here,
You are not two
Any more, but one.

Pity these two
Who all have lost,
Envy these two
Who have paid their cost
To gain this soul
That dazzling hovered
Between them whole
There they are lost

And their tracks are covered;
Nothing can find them
Until they awake
In themselves or take
New selves to bind them.

SONG

Why should your face so please me
That if one little line should stray
Bewilderment would seize me
And drag me down the tortuous way
Out of the noon into the night?
But so, into this tranquil light
You raise me.

How could our minds so marry
That, separate, blunder to and fro,
Make for a point, miscarry,
And blind as headstrong horses go?
Though now they in their promised land
At pleasure travel hand in hand
Or tarry.

This concord is an answer
To questions far beyond our mind
Whose image is a dancer.
All effort is to ease refined
Here, weight is light; this is the dove
Of love and peace, not heartless love
The lancer.

And yet I still must wonder
That such an armistice can be
And life roll by in thunder
To leave this calm with you and me.
This tranquil voice of silence, yes,
This single song of two, this is
A wonder.

SUBURBAN DREAM

Walking the suburbs in the afternoon
In summer when the idle doors stand open
    And the air flows through the rooms
    Fanning the curtain hems,

You wander through a cool elysium
Of women, schoolgirls, children, garden talks,
    With a schoolboy here and there
    Conning his history book.

The men are all away in offices,
Committee-rooms, laboratories, banks,
    Or pushing cotton goods
    In Wick or Ilfracombe.

The massed unanimous absence liberates
The light keys of the piano and sets free
    Chopin and everlasting youth,
    Now, with the masters gone.

And all things turn to images of peace,
The boy curled over his book, the young girl poised
    On the path as if beguiled
    By the silence of a wood.

It is a child's dream of a grown-up world.
But soon the brazen evening clocks will bring
  The tramp of feet and brisk
  Fanfare of motor horns
  And the masters come.

READING IN WARTIME

  Boswell by my bed,
  Tolstoy on my table:
  Though the world has bled
  For four and a half years,
  And wives' and mothers' tears
  Collected would be able
  To water a little field
  Untouched by anger and blood,
  A penitential yield
  Somewhere in the world;
  Though in each latitude
  Armies like forests fall,
  The iniquitous and the good
  Head over heels hurled,
  And confusion over all:
  Boswell's turbulent friend
  And his deafening verbal strife,
  Ivan Ilych's death
  Tell me more about life,
  The meaning and the end
  Of our familiar breath,
  Both being personal,
  Than all the carnage can,
  Retrieve the shape of man,
  Lost and anonymous,

Tell me wherever I look
That not one soul can die
Of this or any clan
Who is not one of us
And has a personal tie
Perhaps to someone now
Searching an ancient book,
Folk-tale or country song
In many and many a tongue,
To find the original face,
The individual soul,
The eye, the lip, the brow
For ever gone from their place,
And gather an image whole.

THE LULLABY

The lullaby has crooned to sleep so many
On all the iron fields in such a clamour,
　　There is astonishment
　　Among the waking.

So quickly these awake were cast in slumber,
Full in the light, then covered thick in shadow,
　　There seemed no time to shed
　　Them from the others.

So deafening the clamour, soft the crooning,
So swift the change and simple the confusion,
　　That these though side by side
　　Were far asunder.

The returning and the unreturning races,
Those who took heed, and those who would not listen
But turned straight towards the dark,
So that there was nothing

To do or say, no greeting on their journey,
Farewell or words at all—these two are haunted
For ever each by each,
In each commingled.

DEJECTION

I do not want to be
Here, there or anywhere;
My melancholy
Folds me beyond the reach of care
As in a valley
Whence long ago I tried to sally,
But dreamt and left my dream upon the air.

And now in lunar pleasure
I watch the undreaming folk of rock and stone
Lie side by side alone
Enjoying their enormous leisure,
That shall continue till the day
When rock and stone are put away;
And feel no more than they the sun that burns
On this unmoving scenery,
Nor count nor care to count the dull returns
Of day and month and year and century
Crowding within the crowding urns.

For every eloquent voice dies in this air
Wafted from anywhere to anywhere
And never counted by the careful clock,
That cannot strike the hour
Of power that will dissolve this power
Until the rock rise up and split the rock.

SONG OF PATIENCE

What use has patience,
Won with such difficulty?
Forced out in such a sigh?

The heart in its stations
Has need of patience,
Holding through night and day
Solitary monologue,
Systole and diastole,
Two surly words that say
Each to each in the breast:
'Solid flesh, fluttering soul,
Troubles and fears, troubles and fears,
Quick hope, long delay,
Where is rest? Where is rest?'
Prologue and epilogue
Reiterated in the breast
For thirty, forty, fifty years.
The heart in its stations
Has need of patience.

Patience wearies of itself,
Impatient patience,
For itself can find no use

But to rehearse upon the shelf
Its hackneyed stations,
And so would end the long abuse,
Make each breath its parting breath,
Die in pain, be born in pain,
And to love at last attain:
Love to whom all things are well,
Love that turns all things to ease,
The life that fleets before the eye,
And the motionless isle of death;
That tunes the tedious miseries
And even patience makes to please;
Love to whom the sorrows tell
Their abysmal dreams and cry:
'Weave the spell! Weave the spell!
Make us well.'

SORROW

I do not want it so,
But since things so are made,
Sorrow, sorrow,
Be you my second trade.
I'll learn the workman's skill
And mould the mass of ill
Until I have it so, or so,
And want it so.

I cannot have it so
Unless I frankly make
A pact with sorrow
For joy and sorrow's sake,

And wring from sorrow's pay
Wealth joy would toss away—
Till both are balanced, so, or so,
And even go.

If it were only so . . .
But right and left I find
Sorrow, sorrow,
And cannot be resigned,
Knowing that we were made
By joy to drive joy's trade
And not to waver to and fro,
But quickly go.

EPITAPH

Into the grave, into the grave with him.
Quick, quick, with dust and stones this dead man cover
Who living was a flickering soul so dim
He was never truly loved nor truly a lover.

Since he was half and half, now let him be
Something entire at last here in this night
Which teaches us its absolute honesty
Who stay between the light and the half-light.

He scarce had room for sorrow, even his own;
His vastest dreams were less than six feet tall;
Free of all joys, he crept in himself alone:
To the grave with this poor image of us all.

If now is Resurrection, then let stay
Only what's ours when this is put away.

COMFORT IN SELF-DESPITE

When in revulsion I detest myself
Thus heartily, myself with myself appal,
And in this mortal rubbish delve and delve,
A dustman damned—perhaps the original

Virtue I'd thought so snugly buried so
May yet be found, else never to be found,
And thus exhumed into the light may grow
After this cruel harrowing of the ground.

For as when I have spoken spitefully
Of this or that friend, piling ill on ill,
Remembrance cleans his image and I see
The pure and touching good no taunt could kill,

So I may yet recover by this bad
Research that good I scarcely dreamt I had.

THE TRANSMUTATION

That all should change to ghost and glance and gleam,
And so transmuted stand beyond all change,
And we be poised between the unmoving dream
And the sole moving moment—this is strange

Past all contrivance, word, or image, or sound,
Or silence, to express, that we who fall
Through time's long ruin should weave this phantom ground
And in its ghostly borders gather all.

There incorruptible the child plays still,
The lover waits beside the trysting tree,
The good hour spans its heaven, and the ill,
Rapt in their silent immortality,

As in commemoration of a day
That having been can never pass away.

TIME HELD IN TIME'S DESPITE

Now there is only left what time has made
Our very own in our and time's despite,
And we ourselves have nothing, but are stayed
By lonely joys and griefs and blank delight.

For this that's ours so surely could not be
But by the word of terror or of grace
That spoke, when all was lost, the guarantee:
'Impersonally soul and soul embrace,

And incorruptibly are bodies bound.'
The hours that melt like snowflakes one by one
Leave us this residue, this virgin ground
For ever fresh, this firmament and this sun.

Then let us lay unasking hand in hand,
And take our way, thus led, into our land.

FOR ANN SCOTT-MONCRIEFF

(1914–1943)

Dear Ann, wherever you are
Since you lately learnt to die,
You are this unsetting star
That shines unchanged in my eye;
So near, inaccessible,
Absent and present so much
Since out of the world you fell,
Fell from hearing and touch—
So near. But your mortal tongue
Used for immortal use,
The grace of a woman young,
The air of an early muse,
The wealth of the chambered brow
And soaring flight of your eyes:
These are no longer now.
Death has a princely prize.

You who were Ann much more
Than others are that or this,
Extravagant over the score
To be what only is,
Would you not still say now
What you once used to say
Of the great Why and How,
On that or the other day?
For though of your heritage
The minority here began,
Now you have come of age
And are entirely Ann.

Under the years' assaults,
In the storm of good and bad,
You too had the faults
That Emily Brontë had,
Ills of body and soul,
Of sinner and saint and all
Who strive to make themselves whole,
Smashed to bits by the Fall.
Yet 'the world is a pleasant place'
I can hear your voice repeat,
While the sun shone in your face
Last summer in Princes Street.

A BIRTHDAY

I never felt so much
Since I have felt at all
The tingling smell and touch
Of dogrose and sweet briar,
Nettles against the wall,
All sours and sweets that grow
Together or apart
In hedge or marsh or ditch.
I gather to my heart
Beast, insect, flower, earth, water, fire,
In absolute desire,
As fifty years ago.

Acceptance, gratitude:
The first look and the last
When all between has passed
Restore ingenuous good

That seeks no personal end,
Nor strives to mar or mend.
Before I touched the food
Sweetness ensnared my tongue;
Before I saw the wood
I loved each nook and bend,
The track going right and wrong;
Before I took the road
Direction ravished my soul.
Now that I can discern
It whole or almost whole,
Acceptance and gratitude
Like travellers return
And stand where first they stood.

ALL WE

All we who make
Things transitory and good
Cannot but take
When walking in a wood
Pleasure in everything
And the maker's solicitude,
Knowing the delicacy
Of bringing shape to birth.
To fashion the transitory
We gave and took the ring
And pledged ourselves to the earth.

IN LOVE FOR LONG

I've been in love for long
With what I cannot tell
And will contrive a song
For the intangible
That has no mould or shape,
From which there's no escape.

It is not even a name,
Yet is all constancy;
Tried or untried, the same,
It cannot part from me;
A breath, yet as still
As the established hill.

It is not any thing,
And yet all being is;
Being, being, being,
Its burden and its bliss.
How can I ever prove
What it is I love?

This happy happy love
Is sieged with crying sorrows,
Crushed beneath and above
Between to-days and morrows;
A little paradise
Held in the world's vice.

And there it is content
And careless as a child,
And in imprisonment
Flourishes sweet and wild;
In wrong, beyond wrong,
All the world's day long.

This love a moment known
For what I do not know
And in a moment gone
Is like the happy doe
That keeps its perfect laws
Between the tiger's paws
And vindicates its cause.

The Labyrinth

1949

TOO MUCH

No, no, I did not bargain for so much
When I set out upon the famous way
My fathers praised so fondly—such and such
The road, the errand, the prize, the part to play.

For everything is different. Hour and place
Are huddled awry, at random teased and tossed,
Too much piled on too much, no track or trace,
And north and south and road and traveller lost.

Then suddenly again I watch the old
Worn saga write across my years and find,
Scene after scene, the tale my fathers told,
But I in the middle blind, as Homer blind,

Dark on the highway, groping in the light,
Threading my dazzling way within my night.

THE LABYRINTH

Since I emerged that day from the labyrinth,
Dazed with the tall and echoing passages,
The swift recoils, so many I almost feared
I'd meet myself returning at some smooth corner,
Myself or my ghost, for all there was unreal
After the straw ceased rustling and the bull
Lay dead upon the straw and I remained,
Blood-splashed, if dead or alive I could not tell
In the twilight nothingness (I might have been
A spirit seeking his body through the roads

Of intricate Hades)—ever since I came out
To the world, the still fields swift with flowers, the trees
All bright with blossom, the little green hills, the sea,
The sky and all in movement under it,
Shepherds and flocks and birds and the young and old,
(I stared in wonder at the young and the old,
For in the maze time had not been with me;
I had strayed, it seemed, past sun and season and change,
Past rest and motion, for I could not tell
At last if I moved or stayed; the maze itself
Revolved around me on its hidden axis
And swept me smoothly to its enemy,
The lovely world)—since I came out that day,
There have been times when I have heard my footsteps
Still echoing in the maze, and all the roads
That run through the noisy world, deceiving streets
That meet and part and meet, and rooms that open
Into each other—and never a final room—
Stairways and corridors and antechambers
That vacantly wait for some great audience,
The smooth sea-tracks that open and close again,
Tracks undiscoverable, indecipherable,
Paths on the earth and tunnels underground,
And bird-tracks in the air—all seemed a part
Of the great labyrinth. And then I'd stumble
In sudden blindness, hasten, almost run,
As if the maze itself were after me
And soon must catch me up. But taking thought,
I'd tell myself, 'You need not hurry. This
Is the firm good earth. All roads lie free before you.'
But my bad spirit would sneer, 'No, do not hurry.
No need to hurry. Haste and delay are equal
In this one world, for there's no exit, none,
No place to come to, and you'll end where you are,
Deep in the centre of the endless maze.'

I could not live if this were not illusion.
It is a world, perhaps; but there's another.
For once in a dream or trance I saw the gods
Each sitting on the top of his mountain-isle,
While down below the little ships sailed by,
Toy multitudes swarmed in the habours, shepherds drove
Their tiny flocks to the pastures, marriage feasts
Went on below, small birthdays and holidays,
Ploughing and harvesting and life and death,
And all permissible, all acceptable,
Clear and secure as in a limpid dream.
But they, the gods, as large and bright as clouds,
Conversed across the sounds in tranquil voices
High in the sky above the untroubled sea,
And their eternal dialogue was peace
Where all these things were woven, and this our life
Was as a chord deep in that dialogue,
As easy utterance of harmonious words,
Spontaneous syllables bodying forth a world.

That was the real world; I have touched it once,
And now shall know it always. But the lie,
The maze, the wild-wood waste of falsehood, roads
That run and run and never reach an end,
Embowered in error—I'd be prisoned there
But that my soul has birdwings to fly free.

Oh these deceits are strong almost as life.
Last night I dreamt I was in the labyrinth,
And woke far on. I did not know the place.

THE WAY

Friend, I have lost the way.
The way leads on.
Is there another way?
The way is one.
I must retrace the track.
It's lost and gone.
Back, I must travel back!
None goes there, none.
Then I'll make here my place,
(*The road runs on*),
Stand still and set my face,
(*The road leaps on*),
Stay here, for ever stay.
None stays here, none.
I cannot find the way.
The way leads on.
Oh places I have passed!
That journey's done.
And what will come at last?
The road leads on.

THE RETURN

I see myself sometimes, an old old man
Who has walked so long with time as time's true servant,
That he's grown strange to me—who was once myself—
Almost as strange as time, and yet familiar
With old man's staff and legendary cloak,
For see, it is I, it is I. And I return
So altered, so adopted, to the house
Of my own life. There all the doors stand open

Perpetually, and the rooms ring with sweet voices,
And there my long life's seasons sound their changes,
Childhood and youth and manhood all together,
And welcome waits, and not a room but is
My own, beloved and longed for. And the voices,
Sweeter than any sound dreamt of or known,
Call me, recall me. I draw near at last,
An old old man, and scan the ancient walls
Rounded and softened by the compassionate years,
The old and heavy and long-leaved trees that watch
This my inheritance in friendly darkness.
And yet I cannot enter, for all within
Rises before me there, rises against me,
A sweet and terrible labyrinth of longing,
So that I turn aside and take the road
That always, early or late, runs on before.

THE WEST

We followed them into the west,
And left them there, and said good-bye. For now
We could go no farther, could not step one step
Beyond the little earthen mound that hid
Their traces from us; for this was an end.
It was as if the west had ended there.
And yet we knew another west ran on,
A west beyond the west, and towards it travelled
Those we had followed to this stopping place.
So we returned by the east and north and south
To our own homes, remembering sometimes there,
Sometimes forgetting, thinking yet not thinking,
Bound by the ancient custom of our country.

But from the east newcomers constantly
Pour in among us, mix with us, pass through us,
And travel towards the west; and that migration
Has been from the beginning, it is said,
And long before men's memory it was woven
Into the tranquil pattern of our lives.
And that great movement like a quiet river,
Which always flowing yet is always the same,
Begets a stillness. So that when we look
Out at our life we see a changeless landscape,
And all disposed there in its due proportion,
The young and old, the good and bad, the wise and foolish,
All these are there as if they had been for ever,
And motionless as statues, prototypes
Set beyond time, for whom the sun stands still.
And each day says in its passing, 'This is all.'—
While the unhurrying progress goes its way,
And we upon it, year by year by year,
Led through the endless stations of the sun.
There are no aborigines in our country,
But all came hither so, and shall leave so,
Even as these friends we followed to their west.

And yet this is a land, and we say 'Now',
Say 'Now' and 'Here', and are in our own house.

THE JOURNEY BACK

I

I take my journey back to seek my kindred,
Old founts dried up whose rivers run far on
Through you and me. Behind, the water-beds
Stone-white with drought; in front the riverless future

Through which our myriad tributaries will wander
When this live patchwork land of green and brown
With all its load of corn and weeds is withered.
But here, but here the water, clear or muddied.

Seek the beginnings, learn from whence you came,
And know the various earth of which you are made.
So I set out on this calm summer evening
From this my house and my father's. Looking back
I see that all behind is pined and shrunken,
The great trees small again, the good walls gone,
The road grown narrow and poor, wild heath and thorn
Where comfortable houses spread their gardens.
Only the sea and sky the same. But quiet
Deeper than I had breathed. Yet in this place,
Most strange and most familiar, my heart says
In a friend's voice, 'I beat in surety;'
My hands grow firm, my father's farmer hands,
And open and shut on surety while I walk
In patient trust. This is my father's gift
Left here for me at the first friendly station
On the long road.
                        But past it all is strange.
I must in other lives with many a leap
Blindfold, must lodge in dark and narrow skulls
With a few thoughts that pad from wall to wall
And never get out, must moulder in dusty hearts,
Inhabit many a dark or a sunny room,
Be in all things. And now I'm locked inside
The savage keep, the grim rectangular tower
From which the fanatic neighbour-hater scowls;
There all is emptiness and dirt and envy,
Dry rubbish of a life in anguish guarded
By mad and watchful eyes. From which I fall
To gasp and choke in the cramped miser's body

That winds its tightening winch to squeeze the soul
In a dry wooden box with slits for eyes.
And when I'm strangling there I flutter out
To drift like gossamer on the sunny wind,
A golden thistledown fool blown here and there,
Who for a lifetime scarcely knows a grief
Or thinks a thought. Then gasp in the hero's breast
That like a spring day in the northern seas
Is storm and shine and thunder all commingled,
A long-linked chain of lightning quenched in night.
Perhaps a murderer next, I watch those hands
That shall be always with me, serve my ends,
Button, unbutton for my body's needs,
Are intimate with me, the officious tools
That wash my face, push food into my mouth,
Loathed servants fed from my averted heart.

So I usurp, grown avid for the end,
Body on body, am both father and child,
Causer and actor, spoiler and despoiled,
Robbing myself, myself, grinding the face
Of the poor, I poorest, who am both rich and poor,
Victor and victim, hapless Many in One.

In all these lives I have lodged, and each a prison.
I fly this prison to seek this other prison,
Impatient for the end—or the beginning
Before the walls were raised, the thick doors fastened,
And there was nothing but the breathing air,
Sun and soft grass, and sweet and vacant ease.
But there's no end, and I could break my journey
Now, here, without a loss, but that some day
I know I shall find a man who has done good
His long lifelong and is
Image of man from whom all have diverged.

The rest is hearsay. So I hie me back
To my sole starting-point, my random self
That in these rags and tatters clothes the soul.

2

Through countless wanderings,
Hastenings, lingerings,
From far I come,
And pass from place to place
In a sleep-wandering pace
To seek my home.

I wear the silver scars
Of blanched and dying stars
Forgotten long,
Whose consternations spread
Terror among the dead
And touched my song.

The well-bred animal
With coat of seemly mail
Was then my guide.
I trembled in my den
With all my kindred when
The dragon died.

Through forests wide and deep
I passed and as a sleep
My wandering was.
Before the word was said
With animal bowed head
I kept the laws.

I thread the shining day;
The mountains as in play
Dizzily turn
My wild road round and round.
No one has seen the ground
For which I burn.

Through countless wanderings,
Hastenings, lingerings,
Nearer I come,
In a sleep-wandering pace
To find the secret place
Where is my home.

3

And I remember in the bright light's maze
While poring on a red and rusted arrow
How once I laid my dead self in the barrow,
Closed my blank eyes and smoothed my face,
And stood aside, a third within that place,
And watched these two at their strange ritual,
And grieved for that day's deed so often done
When the poor child of man, leaving the sun,
Walks out into the sun and goes his way,
Not knowing the resurrection and the life,
Shut in his simple recurring day,
Familiar happiness and ordinary pain.
And while he lives content with child and wife
A million leaves, a million destinies fall,
And over and over again
The red rose blooms and moulders by the wall.

4

And sometimes through the air descends a dust
Blown from the scentless desert of dead time
That whispers: Do not put your trust
In the fed flesh, or colour, or sense, or shape.
This that I am you cannot gather in rhyme.
For once I was all
That you can name, a child, a woman, a flower,
And here escape
From all that was to all,
Lost beyond loss.
So in the air I toss
Remembrance and rememberer all confused
In a light fume, the last power used,
The last form found,
And child and woman and flower
Invisibly fall through the air on the living ground.

I have stood and watched where many have stood
And seen the calamities of an age
Where good seemed evil and evil good
And half the world ran mad to wage
War with an eager heart for the wrong,
War with a bitter heart for the right,
And many, many killed in the fight.

In those days was heard a song:
Blessing upon this time and place,
Blessing upon the disfigured face
And on the cracked and withered tongue
That mouthing a blessing cannot bless,
Blessing upon our helplessness
That, wild for prophecy, is dumb.
Without the blessing cannot the kingdom come.

6

They walk high in their mountainland in light
On winding roads by many a grassy mound
And paths that wander for their own delight.

There they like planets pace their tranquil round
That has no end, whose end is everywhere,
And tread as to a music underground,

An ever-winding and unwinding air
That moves their feet though they in silence go,
For music's self itself has buried there,

And all its tongues in silence overflow
That movement only should be melody.
This is the other road, not that we know.

This is the place of peace, content to be.
All we have seen it; while we look we are
There truly, and even now in memory,

Here on this road, following a falling star.

7

Yet in this journey back
If I should reach the end, if end there was
Before the ever-running roads began
And race and track and runner all were there
Suddenly, always, the great revolving way
Deep in its trance;—if there was ever a place
Where one might say, 'Here is the starting-point,'
And yet not say it, or say it as in a dream,
In idle speculation, imagination,
Reclined at ease, dreaming a life, a way,

And then awaken in the hurtling track,
The great race in full swing far from the start,
No memory of beginning, sign of the end,
And I the dreamer there, a frenzied runner;—
If I should reach that place, how could I come
To where I am but by that deafening road,
Life-wide, world-wide, by which all come to all,
The strong with the weak, the swift with the stationary,
For mountain and man, hunter and quarry there
In tarrying do not tarry, nor hastening hasten,
But all with no division strongly come
For ever to their steady mark, the moment,
And the tumultuous world slips softly home
To its perpetual end and flawless bourne.
How could we be if all were not in all?
Borne hither on all and carried hence with all,
We and the world and that unending thought
Which has elsewhere its end and is for us
Begotten in a dream deep in this dream
Beyond the place of getting and of spending.
There's no prize in this race; the prize is elsewhere,
Here only to be run for. There's no harvest,
Though all around the fields are white with harvest.
There is our journey's ground; we pass unseeing.
But we have watched against the evening sky,
Tranquil and bright, the golden harvester.

THE BRIDGE OF DREAD

But when you reach the Bridge of Dread
Your flesh will huddle into its nest
For refuge and your naked head
Creep in the casement of your breast,

175

And your great bulk grow thin and small
And cower within its cage of bone,
While dazed you watch your footsteps crawl
Toadlike across the leagues of stone.

If they come, you will not feel
About your feet the adders slide,
For still your head's demented wheel
Whirls on your neck from side to side

Searching for danger. Nothing there.
And yet your breath will whistle and beat
As on you push the stagnant air
That breaks in rings about your feet

Like dirty suds. If there should come
Some bodily terror to that place,
Great knotted serpents dread and dumb,
You would accept it as a grace.

Until you see a burning wire
Shoot from the ground. As in a dream
You'll wonder at that flower of fire,
That weed caught in a burning beam.

And you are past. Remember then,
Fix deep within your dreaming head
Year, hour or endless moment when
You reached and crossed the Bridge of Dread.

THE HELMET

The helmet on his head
Has melted flesh and bone
And forged a mask instead
That always is alone.

War has rased its brow
Without a single scar
And left a silent vow
Upon it, like a star.

Its space-devouring eyes
Pass me and hurry on,
Quick as the bullet flies
Until the target's won.

Just now I do not know
What worlds its musings kill . . .
Rivers of sweetness flow
From every little hill;

And we are walking there,
And we are sitting here,
Waiting for what we were
To speak and to appear.

But he can never come home,
Nor I get to the place
Where, tame, the terrors roam
Whose shadows fill his face.

THE CHILD DYING

Unfriendly friendly universe,
I pack your stars into my purse,
And bid you, bid you so farewell.
That I can leave you, quite go out,
Go out, go out beyond all doubt,
My father says, is the miracle.

You are so great, and I so small:
I am nothing, you are all:
Being nothing, I can take this way.
Oh I need neither rise nor fall,
For when I do not move at all
I shall be out of all your day.

It's said some memory will remain
In the other place, grass in the rain,
Light on the land, sun on the sea,
A flitting grace, a phantom face,
But the world is out. There is no place
Where it and its ghost can ever be.

Father, father, I dread this air
Blown from the far side of despair,
The cold cold corner. What house, what hold,
What hand is there? I look and see
Nothing-filled eternity,
And the great round world grows weak and old.

Hold my hand, oh hold it fast—
I am changing!—until at last
My hand in yours no more will change,
Though yours change on. You here, I there,
So hand in hand, twin-leafed despair—
I did not know death was so strange.

THE COMBAT

It was not meant for human eyes,
That combat on the shabby patch
Of clods and trampled turf that lies
Somewhere beneath the sodden skies
For eye of toad or adder to catch.

And having seen it I accuse
The crested animal in his pride,
Arrayed in all the royal hues
Which hide the claws he well can use
To tear the heart out of the side.

Body of leopard, eagle's head
And whetted beak, and lion's mane,
And frost-grey hedge of feathers spread
Behind—he seemed of all things bred.
I shall not see his like again.

As for his enemy, there came in
A soft round beast as brown as clay;
All rent and patched his wretched skin;
A battered bag he might have been,
Some old used thing to throw away.

Yet he awaited face to face
The furious beast and the swift attack.
Soon over and done. That was no place
Or time for chivalry or for grace.
The fury had him on his back.

And two small paws like hands flew out
To right and left as the trees stood by.
One would have said beyond a doubt
This was the very end of the bout,
But that the creature would not die.

For ere the death-stroke he was gone,
Writhed, whirled, huddled into his den,
Safe somehow there. The fight was done,
And he had lost who had all but won.
But oh his deadly fury then.

A while the place lay blank, forlorn,
Drowsing as in relief from pain.
The cricket chirped, the grating thorn
Stirred, and a little sound was born.
The champions took their posts again.

And all began. The stealthy paw
Slashed out and in. Could nothing save
These rags and tatters from the claw?
Nothing. And yet I never saw
A beast so helpless and so brave.

And now, while the trees stand watching, still
The unequal battle rages there.
The killing beast that cannot kill
Swells and swells in his fury till
You'd almost think it was despair.

THE INTERCEPTER

Whatever I do, wherever I go,
This is my everlasting care:
The Intercepter haunts my ways
And checks me everywhere.

I leave him at the end of the street
And wander careless through the lands.
Right in the middle of the road
The Intercepter stands.

When dreaming on the dreaming hills,
I let my thoughts roam far and wide,
The Intercepter lifts his hand
And closes up my side.

Asleep, awake, at work or play,
Whatever I do, wherever I go,
The Intercepter bars my way,
And to my 'Yes' says 'No'.

Is he my friend or my enemy,
Betrayer, saviour from disgrace?
The Intercepter frowns at me
With my own frowning face.

HEAD AND HEART

Our tears have mingled with the rain,
Our cries have vanished on the wind,
Time has carried away our pain.

These are our houses, calm and blind
With permanence of polished stone
That paints indifference on the mind.

Beyond their walls outlawed, alone,
Our muted sorrows smoulder and start,
The lonely tear, the silent groan.

How well they keep themselves apart!
Oh, what we know and what we see
Are separate as head and heart,

And all our sorrow a memory.

THE INTERROGATION

We could have crossed the road but hesitated,
And then came the patrol;
The leader conscientious and intent,
The men surly, indifferent.
While we stood by and waited
The interrogation began. He says the whole
Must come out now, who, what we are,
Where we have come from, with what purpose, whose
Country or camp we plot for or betray.
Question on question.
We have stood and answered through the standing day
And watched across the road beyond the hedge
The careless lovers in pairs go by,
Hand linked in hand, wandering another star,
So near we could shout to them. We cannot choose
Answer or action here,
Though still the careless lovers saunter by
And the thoughtless field is near.
We are on the very edge,
Endurance almost done,
And still the interrogation is going on.

THE BORDER

What shall avail me
When I reach the border?
This staff will fail me,
This pass all in order.

These words I have learned
Will not help me then,
These honours hard earned,
And applause of men.

My harp truly set
Will break string by string;
I shall quite forget
That once I could sing.

Absence pure and cold
Of sense and memory
Lightly will hold
All that is me.

All, all will fail me,
Tongue, foot and hand.
Strange I shall hale me
To that strange land.

THE GOOD TOWN

Look at it well. This was the good town once,
Known everywhere, with streets of friendly neighbours,
Street friend to street and house to house. In summer
All day the doors stood open; lock and key
Were quaint antiquities fit for museums
With gyves and rusty chains. The ivy grew
From post to post across the prison door.
The yard behind was sweet with grass and flowers,
A place where grave philosophers loved to walk.
Old Time that promises and keeps his promise
Was our sole lord indulgent and severe,

Who gave and took away with gradual hand
That never hurried, never tarried, still
Adding, substracting. These our houses had
Long fallen into decay but that we knew
Kindness and courage can repair time's faults,
And serving him breeds patience and courtesy
In us, light sojourners and passing subjects.
There is a virtue in tranquillity
That makes all fitting, childhood and youth and age,
Each in its place.

               Look well. These mounds of rubble,
And shattered piers, half-windows, broken arches
And groping arms were once inwoven in walls
Covered with saints and angels, bore the roof,
Shot up the towering spire. These gaping bridges
Once spanned the quiet river which you see
Beyond that patch of raw and angry earth
Where the new concrete houses sit and stare.
Walk with me by the river. See, the poplars
Still gather quiet gazing on the stream.
The white road winds across the small green hill
And then is lost. These few things still remain.
Some of our houses too, though not what once
Lived there and drew a strength from memory.
Our people have been scattered, or have come
As strangers back to mingle with the strangers
Who occupy our rooms where none can find
The place he knew but settles where he can.
No family now sits at the evening table;
Father and son, mother and child are *out*,
A quaint and obsolete fashion. In our houses
Invaders speak their foreign tongues, informers
Appear and disappear, chance whores, officials
Humble or high, frightened, obsequious,

Sit carefully in corners. My old friends
(Friends ere these great disasters) are dispersed
In parties, armies, camps, conspiracies.
We avoid each other. If you see a man
Who smiles good-day or waves a lordly greeting
Be sure he's a policeman or a spy.
We know them by their free and candid air.

It was not time that brought these things upon us,
But these two wars that trampled on us twice,
Advancing and withdrawing, like a herd
Of clumsy-footed beasts on a stupid errand
Unknown to them or us. Pure chance, pure malice,
Or so it seemed. And when, the first war over,
The armies left and our own men came back
From every point by many a turning road,
Maimed, crippled, changed in body or in mind,
It was a sight to see the cripples come
Out on the fields. The land looked all awry,
The roads ran crooked and the light fell wrong.
Our fields were like a pack of cheating cards
Dealt out at random—all we had to play
In the bad game for the good stake, our life.
We played; a little shrewdness scraped us through.
Then came the second war, passed and repassed,
And now you see our town, the fine new prison,
The house-doors shut and barred, the frightened faces
Peeping round corners, secret police, informers,
And all afraid of all.

                    How did it come?
From outside, so it seemed, an endless source,
Disorder inexhaustible, strange to us,
Incomprehensible. Yet sometimes now
We ask ourselves, we the old citizens:

'Could it have come from us? Was our peace peace?
Our goodness goodness? That old life was easy
And kind and comfortable; but evil is restless
And gives no rest to the cruel or the kind.
How could our town grow wicked in a moment?
What is the answer? Perhaps no more than this,
That once the good men swayed our lives, and those
Who copied them took a while the hue of goodness,
A passing loan; while now the bad are up,
And we, poor ordinary neutral stuff,
Not good nor bad, must ape them as we can,
In sullen rage or vile obsequiousness.
Say there's a balance between good and evil
In things, and it's so mathematical,
So finely reckoned that a jot of either,
A bare preponderance will do all you need,
Make a town good, or make it what you see.
But then, you'll say, only that jot is wanting,
That grain of virtue. No: when evil comes
All things turn adverse, and we must begin
At the beginning, heave the groaning world
Back in its place again, and clamp it there.
Then all is hard and hazardous. We have seen
Good men made evil wrangling with the evil,
Straight minds grown crooked fighting crooked minds.
Our peace betrayed us; we betrayed our peace.
Look at it well. This was the good town once.'

These thoughts we have, walking among our ruins.

THE USURPERS

There is no answer. We do here what we will
And there is no answer. This our liberty
No one has known before, nor could have borne,
For it is rooted in this deepening silence
That is our work and has become our kingdom.
If there were an answer, how could we be free?
It was not hard to still the ancestral voices:
A careless thought, less than a thought could do it.
And the old garrulous ghosts died easily,
The friendly and unfriendly, and are not missed
That once were such proud masters. In this air
Our thoughts are deeds; we dare do all we think,
Since there's no one to check us, here or elsewhere.
All round us stretches nothing; we move through nothing,
Nothing but nothing world without end. We are
Self-guided, self-impelled and self-sustained,
Archer and bow and burning arrow sped
On its wild flight through nothing to tumble down
At last on nothing, our home and cure for all.
Around us is alternate light and darkness.
We live in light and darkness. When night comes
We drop like stones plumb to its ocean ground,
While dreams stream past us upward to the place
Where light meets darkness, place of images,
Forest of ghosts, thicket of muttering voices.
We never seek that place; we are for the day
And for the night alone, at home in both.
But each has its device, and this is night's:
To hide in the very heart of night from night,
Black in its blackness.
                            For these fluttering dreams,
They'd trouble us if we were credulous,
For all the ghosts that frightened frightened men

Long since were bred in that pale territory.
These we can hold in check, but not forget,
Not quite forget, they're so inconsequent.
Sometimes we've heard in sleep tongues talking so:
'I lean my face far out from eternity
For time to work its work on: time, oh time,
What have you done?' These fancies trouble us.
The day itself sometimes works spells upon us
And then the trees look unfamiliar. Yet
It is a lie that they are witnesses,
That the mountains judge us, brooks tell tales about us.
We have thought sometimes the rocks looked strangely on
    us,
Have fancied that the waves were angry with us,
Heard dark runes murmuring in the autumn wind,
Muttering and murmuring like old toothless women
That prophesied against us in ancient tongues.

These are imaginations. We are free.

THE BARGAIN

I knew it! yes, before time told on time
For the first time, or ever I knew time was.
I saw the effect before I marked the cause,
I bore the charge and did not know the crime.

Innocent of deceit, I felt the change,
Perplexed what change could be; my mind and heart
That knew the whole saw part disowned by part
And creep into itself, forlorn and strange.

Time gave and took away. This life it gave;
And life is quick and warm, and death is cold.
It took the story that never can be told,
The unfading light and the unbreaking wave.

I strike the bargain, since time's hand is there;
But having done, this clause I here declare.

OEDIPUS

I, Oedipus, the club-foot, made to stumble,
Who long in the light have walked the world in darkness,
And once in the darkness did that which the light
Found and disowned—too well I have loved the light,
Too dearly have rued the darkness. I am one
Who as in innocent play sought out his guilt,
And now through guilt seeks other innocence,
Beset by evil thoughts, led by the gods.

There was a room, a bed of darkness, once
Known to me, now to all. Yet in that darkness,
Before the light struck, she and I who lay
There without thought of sin and knew each other
Too well, yet were to each other quite unknown
Though fastened mouth to mouth and breast to breast—
Strangers laid on one bed, as children blind,
Clear-eyed and blind as children—did we sin
Then on that bed before the light came on us,
Desiring good to each other, bringing, we thought,
Great good to each other? But neither guilt nor death.

Yet if that darkness had been darker yet,
Buried in endless dark past reach of light
Or eye of the gods, a kingdom of solid darkness

Impregnable and immortal, would we have sinned,
Or lived like the gods in deathless innocence?
For sin is born in the light; therefore we cower
Before the face of the light that none can meet
And all must seek. And when in memory now,
Woven of light and darkness, a stifling web,
I call her back, dear, dreaded, who lay with me,
I see guilt, only guilt, my nostrils choke
With the smell of guilt, and I can scarcely breathe
Here in the guiltless guilt-evoking sun.

And when young Oedipus—for it was Oedipus
And not another—on that long vanished night
Far in my night, at that predestined point
Where three paths like three fates crossed one another,
Tracing the evil figure—when I met
The stranger who menaced me, and flung the stone
That brought him death and me this that I carry,
It was not him but fear I sought to kill,
Fear that, the wise men say, is father of evil,
And was my father in flesh and blood, yet fear,
Fear only, father and fear in one dense body,
So that there was no division, no way past:
Did I sin then, by the gods admonished to sin,
By men enjoined to sin? For it is duty
Of god and man to kill the shapes of fear.

These thoughts recur, vain thoughts. The gods see all,
And will what must be willed, which guards us here.
Their will in them was anger, in me was terror
Long since, but now is peace. For I am led
By them in darkness; light is all about me;
My way lies in the light; they know it; I
Am theirs to guide and hold. And I have learned,
Though blind, to see with something of their sight,
Can look into that other world and watch

King Oedipus the just, crowned and discrowned,
As one may see oneself rise in a dream,
Distant and strange. Even so I see
The meeting at the place where three roads crossed,
And who was there and why, and what was done
That had to be done and paid for. Innocent
The deed that brought the guilt of father-murder. Pure
The embrace on the bed of darkness. Innocent
And guilty. I have wrought and thought in darkness,
And stand here now, an innocent mark of shame,
That so men's guilt might be made manifest
In such a walking riddle—their guilt and mine,
For I've but acted out this fable. I have judged
Myself, obedient to the gods' high judgment,
And seen myself with their pure eyes, have learnt
That all must bear a portion of the wrong
That is driven deep into our fathomless hearts
Past sight or thought; that bearing it we may ease
The immortal burden of the gods who keep
Our natural steps and the earth and skies from harm.

CIRCLE AND SQUARE

'I give you half of me;
No more, lest I should make
A ground for perjury.
For your sake, for my sake,
Half will you take?'

'Half I'll not take nor give,
For he who gives gives all.
By halves you cannot live;
Then let the barrier fall,
In one circle have all.'

191

'A wise and ancient scorner
Said to me once: Beware
The road that has no corner
Where you can linger and stare.
Choose the square.

'And let the circle run
Its dull and fevered race.
You, my dear, are one;
Show your soul in your face;
Maintain your place.

'Give, but have something to give.
No man can want you all.
Live, and learn to live.
When all the barriers fall
You are nothing at all.'

LOVE'S REMORSE

I feel remorse for all that time has done
To you, my love, as if myself, not time,
Had set on you the never-resting sun
And the little deadly days, to work this crime.

For not to guard what by such grace was given,
But leave it for the idle hours to take,
Let autumn bury away our summer heaven:
To such a charge what answer can I make

But the old saw still by the heart retold,
'Love is exempt from time.' And that is true.
But we, the loved and the lover, we grow old;
Only the truth, the truth is always new:

'Eternity alone our wrong can right,
That makes all young again in time's despite.'

LOVE IN TIME'S DESPITE

You who are given to me to time were given
Before through time I stretched my hand to catch
Yours in the flying race. Oh we were driven
By rivalry of him who has no match.

For that cold conqueror, unfeeling lover,
Who robs your deep heart's treasuries as in play,
Trampling your tender harvests over and over,
Where no door is at ease can find his way.

His light embrace is subtle and keen as thought;
Yet, perfect careful lover, he has no care
For you at all, is naught and leaves you naught.

And we who love and love again can dare
To keep in his despite our summer still,
Which flowered, but shall not wither, at his will.

SOLILOQUY

I have seen Alexandria, imperial Rome,
And the sultry backlanes of Jerusalem
One late spring evening thirty years ago
Trouble me still. It was a holy day:
The inns and taverns packed to the very door,
Goods, cattle, families, fellowships, clans;
And some time after a man was crucified,
So it is said, who died for love of the world.
Strange deeds, strange scenes. I have passed through war and
    peace,
Watched populations driven along the roads
To emptiness, movements like bird-migrations
Of races and great families, bare at the last,
Equal in destitution. I have felt
Fear in my throat and fury in my heart,
Dreaded the shadow of the waving palm,
The rustling of the lizard, have been caught
In battles where armies shouted foreign cries,
Fought for strange purposes; and in an eddy
Deep in the slaughter once I watched
A madman sitting happy in the sand,
Rapt in his world. I have seen more than I know.
I was a brisk young merchant, brazen as youth
When youth is brazen. Now I am old and wait
Here in my country house in quiet Greece.
What have I gathered?
                  I have picked up wisdom lying
Disused about the world, available still,
Employable still, small odds and scraps of wisdom,
A miscellaneous lot that yet makes up
A something that is genuine, with a body,
A shape, a character, more than half Platonic
(Greek, should I say?), and yet of practical use.

I have learnt a host of little things, and one
Too great for thinking, scarcely to be borne:
That there's a watershed in human life,
A natural mountain which we have to scale;
And once at the top, our journey all lies downward,
Down the long slope to age and sleep and the end,
(Sadder but easier than the hills of youth,
And sometimes shot with gleams of sunset light).
Oh the air is different on this side of the hill,
The sunset side. And when I breathed it first
I felt dismay so deep and yet so quiet,
It was a silence rather, a sea of silence.
This is my trouble, the common trouble.

                             I have seen
Troy's harbour deep in the fields with turf grown over
And poppies nodding on the rustic quays;
And temples and curious caverns in the rocks
Scrawled thick with suns and birds and animals,
Fruit, fire and feast, flower-garlanded underworld;
Past reading.

                        I have learned another lesson:
When life's half done you must give quality
To the other half, else you lose both, lose all.
Select, select: make an anthology
Of what's been given you by bold casual time.
Revise, omit; keep what's significant.
Fill, fill deserted time. Oh there's no comfort
In the wastes of empty time. Provide for age.
Life must be lived; then live. And so I turn
To past experience, watch it being shaped,
But never to its own true shape. However,
I have fitted this or that into the pattern,
Caught sight sometimes of the original

That is myself—should rather be myself—
The soul past price bartered at any price
The moment bids, cheap as the cheapest moment.
I have had such glimpses, made such tentative
Essays to shape my life, have had successes,
Whether real or apparent time may tell,
Though there's no bargain you can drive with time.
All this is insufficient.

                                    I have watched
In cheering ports the great fleets setting out,
And on another and a darker day
Returning with disaster at the helm,
Death at the prow—and then the punishments,
The crucifixions on the burning hills,
Hour-long day-long slow death. And once I came
Upon the gaunt-ribbed skeleton of a wreck
Black underneath the toothed black promontory;
Nothing but these to comfort one another,
And the spray and grinding sea.

                                   I have seen such things.
I have begotten life and taken away
Life lent to others. I have thought of death,
And followed Plato to eternity,
Walked in his radiant world; have trod the fields
My fathers' sins have trampled richly down,
Loam warmed by a sun that burns at the world's heart,
Sol of the underworld. My heart is steady,
Beats in my breast and cannot burn or break,
Systole and diastole for seventy years.

Set up the bleak worn day to show our sins,
Old and still ageing, like a flat squat herd
Crawling like sun on wall to the rim of time,
Up the long slope for ever.

                                        Light and praise,
Love and atonement, harmony and peace,
Touch me, assail me; break and make my heart.

THE ABSENT

They are not here. And we, we are the Others
Who walk by ourselves unquestioned in the sun
Which shines for us and only for us.
For They are not here.
And are made known to us in this great absence
That lies upon us and is between us
Since They are not here.
Now, in this kingdom of summer idleness
Where slowly we the sun-tranced multitudes dream and wander
In deep oblivion of brightness
And breathe ourselves out, out into the air—
It is absence that receives us;
We do not touch, our souls go out in the absence
That lies between us and is about us.
For we are the Others,
And so we sorrow for These that are not with us,
Not knowing we sorrow or that this is our sorrow,
Since it is long past thought or memory or device of mourning,
Sorrow for loss of that which we never possessed,
The unknown, the nameless,
The ever-present that in their absence are with us
(With us the inheritors, the usurpers claiming
The sun and the kingdom of the sun) that sorrow
And loneliness might bring a blessing upon us.

THE VISITOR

No, no, do not beguile me, do not come
Between me and my ghost, that cannot move
Till you are gone,
And while you gossip must be dumb.
Do not believe I do not want your love,
Brother and sister, wife and son.
But I would be alone
Now, now and let him in,
Lest while I speak he is already flown,
Offended by the din
Of this half-uttered scarcely whispered plea
(So delicate is he).
No more, no more.
Let the great tidings stay unsaid,
For I must to the door,
And oh I dread
He may even now be gone
Or, when I open, will not enter in.

THE TRANSFIGURATION

So from the ground we felt that virtue branch
Through all our veins till we were whole, our wrists
As fresh and pure as water from a well,
Our hands made new to handle holy things,
The source of all our seeing rinsed and cleansed
Till earth and light and water entering there
Gave back to us the clear unfallen world.
We would have thrown our clothes away for lightness,
But that even they, though sour and travel stained,
Seemed, like our flesh, made of immortal substance,

198

And the soiled flax and wool lay light upon us
Like friendly wonders, flower and flock entwined
As in a morning field. Was it a vision?
Or did we see that day the unseeable
One glory of the everlasting world
Perpetually at work, though never seen
Since Eden locked the gate that's everywhere
And nowhere? Was the change in us alone,
And the enormous earth still left forlorn,
An exile or a prisoner? Yet the world
We saw that day made this unreal, for all
Was in its place. The painted animals
Assembled there in gentle congregations,
Or sought apart their leafy oratories,
Or walked in peace, the wild and tame together,
As if, also for them, the day had come.
The shepherds' hovels shone, for underneath
The soot we saw the stone clean at the heart
As on the starting-day. The refuse heaps
Were grained with that fine dust that made the world;
For he had said, 'To the pure all things are pure.'
And when we went into the town, he with us,
The lurkers under doorways, murderers,
With rags tied round their feet for silence, came
Out of themselves to us and were with us,
And those who hide within the labyrinth
Of their own loneliness and greatness came,
And those entangled in their own devices,
The silent and the garrulous liars, all
Stepped out of their dungeons and were free.
Reality or vision, this we have seen.
If it had lasted but another moment
It might have held for ever! But the world
Rolled back into its place, and we are here,
And all that radiant kingdom lies forlorn,

As if it had never stirred; no human voice
Is heard among its meadows, but it speaks
To itself alone, alone it flowers and shines
And blossoms for itself while time runs on.

But he will come again, it's said, though not
Unwanted and unsummoned; for all things,
Beasts of the field, and woods, and rocks, and seas,
And all mankind from end to end of the earth
Will call him with one voice. In our own time,
Some say, or at a time when time is ripe.
Then he will come, Christ the uncrucified,
Christ the discrucified, his death undone,
His agony unmade, his cross dismantled—
Glad to be so—and the tormented wood
Will cure its hurt and grow into a tree
In a green springing corner of young Eden,
And Judas damned take his long journey backward
From darkness into light and be a child
Beside his mother's knee, and the betrayal
Be quite undone and never more be done.

THE DEBTOR

I am debtor to all, to all am I bounden,
Fellowman and beast, season and solstice, darkness and light,
And life and death. On the backs of the dead,
See, I am borne, on lost errands led,
By spent harvests nourished. Forgotten prayers
To gods forgotten bring blessings upon me.
Rusted arrow and broken bow, look, they preserve me
Here in this place. The never-won stronghold
That sank in the ground as the years into time,

Slowly with all its men steadfast and watching,
Keeps me safe now. The ancient waters
Cleanse me, revive me. Victor and vanquished
Give me their passion, their peace and the field.
The meadows of Lethe shed twilight around me.
The dead in their silences keep me in memory,
Have me in hold. To all I am bounden.

SONG

Sunset ends the day,
The years shift their place,
Under the sun's sway
Times from times fall;
Mind fighting mind
The secret cords unwind
No power can replace:
Love gathers all.

The living and the dead
Centuries separate,
Man from himself is led
Through mazes past recall,
Distraction can disguise
The wastrel and the wise
Till neither knows his state:
Love gathers all.

Father at odds with son
Breeds ageless enmity,
Friendships undone
Build up a topless wall;

Achilles and Hector slain
Fight, fight and fight again
In measureless memory:
Love gathers all.

The quarrel from the start,
Long past and never past,
The war of mind and heart,
The great war and the small
That tumbles the hovel down
And topples town on town
Come to one place at last:
Love gathers all.

THE TOY HORSE

See him, the gentle Bible beast,
With lacquered hoofs and curling mane,
His wondering journey from the East
Half done, between the rock and plain,

His little kingdom at his feet
Through which the silver rivulets flow,
For while his hoofs in silence beat
Beside him Eden and Canaan go.

The great leaves turn and then are still.
Page after page through deepening day
He steps, and from each morning hill
Beholds his stationary way.

His lifted foot commands the West,
And, lingering, halts the turning sun;
Endless departure, endless rest,
End and beginning here are one.

Dumb wooden idol, you have led
Millions on your calm pilgrimage
Between the living and the dead,
And shine yet in your golden age.

One Foot in Eden

1956

Part I

MILTON

Milton, his face set fair for Paradise,
And knowing that he and Paradise were lost
In separate desolation, bravely crossed
Into his second night and paid his price.
There towards the end he to the dark tower came
Set square in the gate, a mass of blackened stone
Crowned with vermilion fiends like streamers blown
From a great funnel filled with roaring flame.

Shut in his darkness, these he could not see,
But heard the steely clamour known too well
On Saturday nights in every street in Hell.
Where, past the devilish din, could Paradise be?
A footstep more, and his unblinded eyes
Saw far and near the fields of Paradise.

THE ANIMALS

They do not live in the world,
Are not in time and space.
From birth to death hurled
No word do they have, not one
To plant a foot upon,
Were never in any place.

For with names the world was called
Out of the empty air,
With names was built and walled,
Line and circle and square,
Dust and emerald;
Snatched from deceiving death
By the articulate breath.

But these have never trod
Twice the familiar track,
Never never turned back
Into the memoried day.
All is new and near
In the unchanging Here
Of the fifth great day of God,
That shall remain the same,
Never shall pass away.

On the sixth day we came.

THE DAYS

Issuing from the Word
The seven days came,
Each in its own place,
Its own name.
And the first long days
A hard and rocky spring,
Inhuman burgeoning,
And nothing there for claw or hand,
Vast loneliness ere loneliness began,
Where the blank seasons in their journeying
Saw water at play with water and sand with sand.

The waters stirred
And from the doors were cast
Wild lights and shadows on the formless face
Of the flood of chaos, vast
Lengthening and dwindling image of earth and heaven.
The forest's green shadow
Softly over the water driven,
As if the earth's green wonder, endless meadow
Floated and sank within its own green light.
In water and night
Sudden appeared the lion's violent head,
Raging and burning in its watery cave.
The stallion's tread
Soundlessly fell on the flood, and the animals poured
Onward, flowing across the flowing wave.
Then on the waters fell
The shadow of man, and earth and the heavens scrawled
With names, as if each pebble and leaf would tell
The tale untellable. And the Lord called
The seventh day forth and the glory of the Lord.
And now we see in the sun
The mountains standing clear in the third day
(Where they shall always stay)
And thence a river run,
Threading, clear cord of water, all to all:
The wooded hill and the cattle in the meadow,
The tall wave breaking on the high sea-wall,
The people at evening walking,
The crescent shadow
Of the light-built bridge, the hunter stalking
The flying quarry, each in a different morning,
The fish in the billow's heart, the man with the net,
The hungry swords crossed in the cross of warning,
The lion set
High on the banner, leaping into the sky,

The seasons playing
Their game of sun and moon and east and west,
The animal watching man and bird go by,
The women praying
For the passing of this fragmentary day
Into the day where all are gathered together,
Things and their names, in the storm's and the lightning's nest,
The seventh great day and the clear eternal weather.

ADAM'S DREAM

They say the first dream Adam our father had
After his agelong daydream in the Garden
When heaven and sun woke in his wakening mind,
The earth with all its hills and woods and waters,
The friendly tribes of trees and animals,
And earth's last wonder Eve (the first great dream
Which is the ground of every dream since then)—
They say he dreamt lying on the naked ground,
The gates shut fast behind him as he lay
Fallen in Eve's fallen arms, his terror drowned
In her engulfing terror, in the abyss
Whence there's no further fall, and comfort is—
That he was standing on a rocky ledge
High on the mountainside, bare crag behind,
In front a plain as far as eye could reach,
And on the plain a few small figures running
That were like men and women, yet were so far away
He could not see their faces. On they ran,
And fell, and rose again, and ran, and fell,
And rising were the same yet not the same,
Identical or interchangeable,
Different in indifference. As he looked

Still there were more of them, the plain was filling
As by an alien arithmetical magic
Unknown in Eden, a mechanical
Addition without meaning, joining only
Number to number in no mode or order,
Weaving no pattern. For these creatures moved
Towards no fixed mark even when in growing bands
They clashed against each other and clashing fell
In mounds of bodies. For they rose again,
Identical or interchangeable,
And went their way that was not like a way;
Some back and forward, back and forward, some
In a closed circle, wide or narrow, others
In zigzags on the sand. Yet all were busy,
And tense with purpose as they cut the air
Which seemed to press them back. Sometimes they paused
While one stopped one—fortuitous assignations
In the disorder, whereafter two by two
They ran awhile,
Then parted and again were single. Some
Ran straight against the frontier of the plain
Till the horizon drove them back. A few
Stood still and never moved. Then Adam cried
Out of his dream, 'What are you doing there?'
And the crag answered 'Are you doing there?'
'What are you doing there?'—'you doing there?'
The animals had withdrawn and from the caves
And woods stared out in fear or condemnation,
Like outlaws or like judges. All at once
Dreaming or half-remembering, 'This is time',
Thought Adam in his dream, and time was strange
To one lately in Eden. 'I must see',
He cried, 'the faces. Where are the faces? Who
Are you all out there?' Then in his changing dream
He was a little nearer, and he saw

They were about some business strange to him
That had a form and sequence past their knowledge;
And that was why they ran so frenziedly.
Yet all, it seemed, made up a story, illustrated
By these the living, the unknowing, cast
Each singly for his part. But Adam longed
For more, not this mere moving pattern, not
This illustrated storybook of mankind
Always a-making, improvised on nothing.
At that he was among them, and saw each face
Was like his face, so that he would have hailed them
As sons of God but that something restrained him.
And he remembered all, Eden, the Fall,
The Promise, and his place, and took their hands
That were his hands, his and his children's hands,
Cried out and was at peace, and turned again
In love and grief in Eve's encircling arms.

OUTSIDE EDEN

A few lead in their harvest still
By the ruined wall and broken gate.
Far inland shines the radiant hill.
Inviolable the empty gate,
Impassable the gaping wall;
And the mountain over all.

Such is the country of this clan,
Haunted by guilt and innocence.
There is a sweetness in the air
That bloomed as soon as time began,
But now is dying everywhere.
This people guard in reverence

Their proud and famous family tree
Sprung from a glorious king who once
Lived in such boundless liberty
As never a one among the great
Has known in all the kingdoms since;
For death was barred from his estate.
Lost long ago, the histories say,
He and his consort lost it all.
Guiltiest and least guilty, they
In innocence discovered sin
Round a lost corner of the day,
And fell and fell through all the fall
That hurled them headlong over the wall.
Their children live where then they lay.

Guilt is next door to innocence.
So here this people choose to live
And never think to travel hence,
Nor learn to be inquisitive,
Nor browse in sin's great library,
The single never-ending book
That fills the shelves of all the earth.
There the learned enquirers look
And blind themselves to see their face.
But these live in the land of birth
And count all else an idle grace.

The simple have long memories.
Memory makes simple all that is.
So these the lawless world can love
At ease, the thickets running wild,
The thorny waste, the flourishing grove.
Their knotted landscape, wrong and clear
As the crude drawings of a child,
Is to them become more dear

Than geometrical symmetry.
Their griefs are all in memory grown
As natural as a weathered stone.
Their troubles are a tribute given
Freely while gazing at the hill.
Such is their simplicity,
Standing on earth, looking at heaven.

PROMETHEUS

The careless seasons pass and leave me here.
The forests rise like ghosts and fade like dreams.
All has its term; flowers flicker on the ground
A summer moment, and the rock is bare.
Alone the animals trace their changeless figure,
Embodying change. Agelong I watch the leopard
Glaring at something past the end of time,
And the wild goat immobile on his rock,
Lost in a trance of roaming through the skies:
I look and he is there. But pilgrim man
Travels foreknowing to his stopping place,
Awareness on his lips, which have tasted sorrow,
Foretasted death. These strangers do not know
Their happiness is in that which leads their sorrow
Round to an end. My hope is not like theirs.
I pray for the end of all things and this pain
Which makes me cry: Move faster, sun and stars,
And bear these chains and bear this body away
Into your flying circuit; freedom waits
There in the blessed nothingness that follows
The charging onset of the centaur-stars,
Trampling time out. For when these clamorous races
Lie silent in the ground from which they came,

And all the earth is quiet, a hush may fall
Even in the house of heaven, and the heedless gods
May raise their eyes to look and bid me come
Again among them, then when the feud is over
And fire and those in whom it blazed and died
Are strewn in ashes on the ashen hills.

What shall I say to the gods? Heaven will be strange,
And strange those scars inscribed in distant time.
Who will give answer to the earth's dark story?
Zeus with the ponderous glory of the bull,
Or the boy Eros with his fretful quiver?
What expectation there except at most
That this my knowledge will be an aeon's gossip?

The shrines are emptying and the peoples changing.
It may be I should find Olympus vacant
If I should return. For I have heard a wonder:
Lands without gods; nothing but earth and water;
Words without mystery; and the only creed
An iron text to beat the round skulls flat
And fit them for the cap of a buried master.
Strange ritual. Now time's storm is rising, sweeping
The sons of man into an emptier room,
Vast as a continent, bare as a desert,
Where the dust takes man's lifetime to revolve
Around the walls, harried by peevish gusts
And little spiteful eddies; nothing standing
But the cast-iron cities and rubbish mountains.

At the world's end to whom shall I tell the story?
A god came down, they say, from another heaven
Not in rebellion but in pity and love,
Was born a son of woman, lived and died,
And rose again with all the spoils of time

Back to his home, where now they are transmuted
Into bright toys and various frames of glory;
And time itself is there a world of marvels.
If I could find that god, he would hear and answer.

THE GRAVE OF PROMETHEUS

No one comes here now, neither god nor man.
For long the animals have kept away,
Scared by immortal cries and the scream of vultures;
Now by this silence. The heavenly thief who stole
Heaven's dangerous treasure turned to common earth
When that great company forsook Olympus.
The fire was out, and he became his barrow.
Ten yards long there he lay outstretched, and grass
Grew over him: all else in a breath forgotten.
Yet there you still may see a tongue of stone,
Shaped like a calloused hand where no hand should be,
Extended from the sward as if for alms,
Its palm all licked and blackened as with fire.
A mineral change made cool his fiery bed,
And made his burning body a quiet mound,
And his great face a vacant ring of daisies.

ORPHEUS' DREAM

And she was there. The little boat
Coasting the perilous isles of sleep,
Zones of oblivion and despair,
Stopped, for Eurydice was there.
The foundering skiff could scarcely keep
All that felicity afloat.

As if we had left earth's frontier wood
Long since and from this sea had won
The lost original of the soul,
The moment gave us pure and whole
Each back to each, and swept us on
Past every choice to boundless good.

Forgiveness, truth, atonement, all
Our love at once—till we could dare
At last to turn our heads and see
The poor ghost of Eurydice
Still sitting in her silver chair,
Alone in Hades' empty hall.

THE OTHER OEDIPUS

Remembered on the Peloponnesian roads,
He and his serving-boy and his concubine,
White-headed and light-hearted, their true wits gone
Past the last stroke of time into a day
Without a yesterday or a to-morrow,
A brightness laid like a blue lake around them,
Or endless field to play or linger in.
They were so gay and innocent, you'd have thought
A god had won a glorious prize for them
In some celestial field, and the odds were gone,
Fate sent on holiday, the earth and heaven
Thenceforth in endless friendly talk together.
They were quite storyless and had clean forgotten
That memory burning in another world;
But they too leaf-light now for any story.
If anyone spoke a word of other guilt
By chance before them, then they stamped their feet

In rage and gnashed their teeth like peevish children.
But then forgot. The road their welcoming home.
They would not stay in a house or let a door
Be shut on them. The surly Spartan farmers
Were kind to them, pitying their happiness.

THE CHARM

There was a drug that Helen knew.
Dropped in the wine-cup it could take
All memory and all grief away,
And while the drinker, wide awake,
Sat in his chair, indifference grew
Around him in the estranging day.
He saw the colours shine and flow,
The giant lineaments break and change,
But all storyless, all strange.
The crystal spheres on Helen's brow
Took and gave back the coloured world,
Yet only seemed to smile or glare
At nothing but the empty air.
The serving women crossed the floor,
Swept by a silent tempest, whirled
Into the light and through the door.
This he saw and nothing more,
While all the charities, unborn,
Slept soundly in his burdened breast
As he took his heavy rest,
Careless, thoughtless and forlorn.

So strong the enchantment, Homer says,
That if this man's own son had died,
Killed at his feet, his dreaming gaze

(Like a false-hearted summer day
Watching the hunter and his prey
At ease) would not have changed at all,
Nor his heart knocked against his side.
But far within him something cried
For the great tragedy to start,
The pang in lingering mercy fall,
And sorrow break upon his heart.

TELEMACHOS REMEMBERS

Twenty years, every day,
The figures in the web she wove
Came and stood and went away.
Her fingers in their pitiless play
Beat downward as the shuttle drove.

Slowly, slowly did they come,
With horse and chariot, spear and bow,
Half-finished heroes sad and mum,
Came slowly to the shuttle's hum.
Time itself was not so slow.

And what at last was there to see?
A horse's head, a trunkless man,
Mere odds and ends about to be,
And the thin line of augury
Where through the web the shuttle ran.

How could she bear the mounting load,
Dare once again her ghosts to rouse?
Far away Odysseus trod
The treadmill of the turning road
That did not bring him to his house.

The weary loom, the weary loom,
The task grown sick from morn to night,
From year to year. The treadle's boom
Made a low thunder in the room.
The woven phantoms mazed her sight.

If she had pushed it to the end,
Followed the shuttle's cunning song
So far she had no thought to rend
In time the web from end to end,
She would have worked a matchless wrong.

Instead, that jumble of heads and spears,
Forlorn scraps of her treasure trove.
I wet them with my childish tears
Not knowing she wove into her fears
Pride and fidelity and love.

THE HEROES

When these in all their bravery took the knock
And like obedient children swaddled and bound
Were borne to sleep within the chambered rock,
A splendour broke from that impervious ground,
Which they would never know. Whence came that greatness?
No fiery chariot whirled them heavenwards, they
Saw no Elysium opening, but the straitness
Of full submission bound them where they lay.

What could that greatness be? It was not fame.
Yet now they seemed to grow as they grew less,
And where they lay were more than where they had stood.
They did not go to any beatitude.
They were stripped clean of feature, presence, name,
When that strange glory broke from namelessness.

ABRAHAM

The rivulet-loving wanderer Abraham
Through waterless wastes tracing his fields of pasture
Led his Chaldean herds and fattening flocks
With the meandering art of wavering water
That seeks and finds, yet does not know its way.
He came, rested and prospered, and went on,
Scattering behind him little pastoral kingdoms,
And over each one its own particular sky,
Not the great rounded sky through which he journeyed,
That went with him but when he rested changed.
His mind was full of names
Learned from strange peoples speaking alien tongues,
And all that was theirs one day he would inherit.
He died content and full of years, though still
The Promise had not come, and left his bones,
Far from his father's house, in alien Canaan.

THE SUCCESSION

Legendary Abraham,
The old Chaldean wanderer,
First among these peoples came,
Cruising above them like a star
That is in love with distances
And has through age to calmness grown,
Patient in the wilderness
And untarrying in the sown.
At last approached his setting mark.
Thence he sent his twin star out,
Isaac, to revolve alone.
For two great stars that through an age

Play in their corner of the sky,
Separate go into the dark,
And ere they end their roundabout
One must live and one must die.

Isaac in his tutelage
Wheeled around the father light.
Then began his pilgrimage
Through another day and night,
Other peoples, other lands.
Where the father could not go
There is gone the careless son.
He can never miss his way.
By strangers' hands to strangers' hands
He is carried where he will.
Free, he must the powers obey,
Serve, be served by good and ill,
Safe through all the hazards run.
All shall watch him come and go
Until his quittance he has won;
And Jacob wheels into the day.

We through the generations came
Here by a way we do not know
From the fields of Abraham,
And still the road is scarce begun.
To hazard and to danger go
The sallying generations all
Where the imperial highways run.
And our songs and legends call
The hazard and the danger good;
For our fathers understood
That danger was by hope begot
And hazard by revolving chance
Since first we drew the enormous lot.

THE ROAD

The great road stretched before them, clear and still,
Then from in front one cried: 'Turn back! Turn back!'
Yet they had never seen so fine a track,
Honest and frank past any thought of ill.
But when they glanced behind, how strange, how strange,
These wild demented windings in and out—
Traced by some devil of mischief or of doubt?—
That was the road they had come by. Could it change?

How could they penetrate that perilous maze
Backwards, again, climb backwards down the scree
From the wrong side, slither among the dead?
Yet as they travelled on, for many days
These words rang in their ears as if they said,
'There was another road you did not see.'

THE ANNUNCIATION

The angel and the girl are met.
Earth was the only meeting place.
For the embodied never yet
Travelled beyond the shore of space.
The eternal spirits in freedom go.

See, they have come together, see,
While the destroying minutes flow,
Each reflects the other's face
Till heaven in hers and earth in his
Shine steady there. He's come to her
From far beyond the farthest star,
Feathered through time. Immediacy

Of strangest strangeness is the bliss
That from their limbs all movement takes.
Yet the increasing rapture brings
So great a wonder that it makes
Each feather tremble on his wings.

Outside the window footsteps fall
Into the ordinary day
And with the sun along the wall
Pursue their unreturning way.
Sound's perpetual roundabout
Rolls its numbered octaves out
And hoarsely grinds its battered tune.

But through the endless afternoon
These neither speak nor movement make,
But stare into their deepening trance
As if their gaze would never break.

THE KILLING

That was the day they killed the Son of God
On a squat hill-top by Jerusalem.
Zion was bare, her children from their maze
Sucked by the demon curiosity
Clean through the gates. The very halt and blind
Had somehow got themselves up to the hill.

After the ceremonial preparation,
The scourging, nailing, nailing against the wood,
Erection of the main-trees with their burden,
While from the hill rose an orchestral wailing,
They were there at last, high up in the soft spring day.

We watched the writhings, heard the moanings, saw
The three heads turning on their separate axles
Like broken wheels left spinning. Round *his* head
Was loosely bound a crown of plaited thorn
That hurt at random, stinging temple and brow
As the pain swung into its envious circle.
In front the wreath was gathered in a knot
That as he gazed looked like the last stump left
Of a death-wounded deer's great antlers. Some
Who came to stare grew silent as they looked,
Indignant or sorry. But the hardened old
And the hard-hearted young, although at odds
From the first morning, cursed him with one curse,
Having prayed for a Rabbi or an armed Messiah
And found the Son of God. What use to them
Was a God or a Son of God? Of what avail
For purposes such as theirs? Beside the cross-foot,
Alone, four women stood and did not move
All day. The sun revolved, the shadow wheeled,
The evening fell. His head lay on his breast,
But in his breast they watched his heart move on
By itself alone, accomplishing its journey.
Their taunts grew louder, sharpened by the knowledge
That he was walking in the park of death,
Far from their rage. Yet all grew stale at last,
Spite, curiosity, envy, hate itself.
They waited only for death and death was slow
And came so quietly they scarce could mark it.
They were angry then with death and death's deceit.

I was a stranger, could not read these people
Or this outlandish deity. Did a God
Indeed in dying cross my life that day
By chance, he on his road and I on mine?

ANTICHRIST

He walks, the enchanter, on his sea of glass,
Poring upon his blue inverted heaven
Where a false sun revolves from west to east.
If he could raise his eyes he would see his hell.
He is no spirit, nor a spirit's shadow,
But a mere toy shaped by ingenious devils
To bring discomfiture on credulous man.
He's the false copy where each feature's wrong,
Yet so disposed the whole gives a resemblance.
When he's in anguish smiles writhe on his lips
And will not stop. His imperturbable brow
Is carved by rage not his but theirs that made him,
For he's a nothing where they move in freedom,
Knowing that nothing's there. When he forgives
It is for love of sin not of the sinner.
He takes sin for his province, knows sin only,
Nothing but sin from end to end of the world.
He heals the sick to show his conjuring skill,
Vexed only by the cure; and turns his cheek
To goad the furious to more deadly fury,
And damn by a juggling trick the ingenuous sinner.
He brings men from the dead to tell the living
That their undoing is a common fetch.
Ingeniously he postures on the Tree
(His crowning jest), an actor miming death,
While his indifferent mind is idly pleased
That treason should run on through time for ever.
His vast indulgence is so free and ample,
You well might think it universal love,
For all seems goodness, sweetness, harmony.
He is the Lie; one true thought, and he's gone.

ONE FOOT IN EDEN

One foot in Eden still, I stand
And look across the other land.
The world's great day is growing late,
Yet strange these fields that we have planted
So long with crops of love and hate.
Time's handiworks by time are haunted,
And nothing now can separate
The corn and tares compactly grown.
The armorial weed in stillness bound
About the stalk; these are our own.
Evil and good stand thick around
In the fields of charity and sin
Where we shall lead our harvest in.

Yet still from Eden springs the root
As clean as on the starting day.
Time takes the foliage and the fruit
And burns the archetypal leaf
To shapes of terror and of grief
Scattered along the winter way.
But famished field and blackened tree
Bear flowers in Eden never known.
Blossoms of grief and charity
Bloom in these darkened fields alone.
What had Eden ever to say
Of hope and faith and pity and love
Until was buried all its day
And memory found its treasure trove?
Strange blessings never in Paradise
Fall from these beclouded skies.

THE INCARNATE ONE

The windless northern surge, the sea-gull's scream,
And Calvin's kirk crowning the barren brae.
I think of Giotto the Tuscan shepherd's dream,
Christ, man and creature in their inner day.
How could our race betray
The Image, and the Incarnate One unmake
Who chose this form and fashion for our sake?

The Word made flesh here is made word again,
A word made word in flourish and arrogant crook.
See there King Calvin with his iron pen,
And God three angry letters in a book,
And there the logical hook
On which the Mystery is impaled and bent
Into an ideological instrument.

There's better gospel in man's natural tongue,
And truer sight was theirs outside the Law
Who saw the far side of the Cross among
The archaic peoples in their ancient awe,
In ignorant wonder saw
The wooden cross-tree on the bare hillside,
Not knowing that there a God suffered and died.

The fleshless word, growing, will bring us down,
Pagan and Christian man alike will fall,
The auguries say, the white and black and brown,
The merry and sad, theorist, lover, all
Invisibly will fall:
Abstract calamity, save for those who can
Build their cold empire on the abstract man.

A soft breeze stirs and all my thoughts are blown
Far out to sea and lost. Yet I know well
The bloodless word will battle for its own
Invisibly in brain and nerve and cell.
The generations tell
Their personal tale: the One has far to go
Past the mirages and the murdering snow.

SCOTLAND'S WINTER

Now the ice lays its smooth claws on the sill,
The sun looks from the hill
Helmed in his winter casket,
And sweeps his arctic sword across the sky.
The water at the mill
Sounds more hoarse and dull.
The miller's daughter walking by
With frozen fingers soldered to her basket
Seems to be knocking
Upon a hundred leagues of floor
With her light heels, and mocking
Percy and Douglas dead,
And Bruce on his burial bed,
Where he lies white as may
With wars and leprosy,
And all the kings before
This land was kingless,
And all the singers before
This land was songless,
This land that with its dead and living waits the Judgment Day.
But they, the powerless dead,
Listening can hear no more
Than a hard tapping on the sounding floor

A little overhead
Of common heels that do not know
Whence they come or where they go
And are content
With their poor frozen life and shallow banishment.

THE GREAT HOUSE

However it came, this great house has gone down
Unconquered into chaos (as you might see
A famous ship warped to a rotting quay
In miles of weeds and rubbish, once a town.)
So the great house confronts the brutish air,
And points its turrets towards the hidden sky,
While in the dark the flags of honour fly
Where faith and hope and bravery would not dare.

Accident did not do this, nor mischance.
But so must order to disorder come
At their due time, and honour take its stance
Deep in dishonour's ground. Chaos is new,
And has no past or future. Praise the few
Who built in chaos our bastion and our home.

THE EMBLEM

I who so carefully keep in such repair
The six-inch king and the toy treasury,
Prince, poet, realm shrivelled in time's black air,
I am not, although I seem, an antiquary.
For that scant-acre kingdom is not dead,

Nor save in seeming shrunk. When at its gate,
Which you pass daily, you incline your head,
And enter (do not knock; it keeps no state)

You will be with space and order magistral,
And that contracted world so vast will grow
That this will seem a little tangled field.
For you will be in very truth with all
In their due place and honour, row on row.
For this I read the emblem on the shield.

Part II

TO FRANZ KAFKA

If we, the proximate damned, presumptive blest,
Were called one day to some high consultation
With the authentic ones, the worst and best
Picked from all time, how mean would be our station.
Oh we could never bear the standing shame,
Equivocal ignominy of non-election;
We who will hardly answer to our name,
And on the road direct ignore direction.

But you, dear Franz, sad champion of the drab
And half, would watch the tell-tale shames drift in
(As if they were troves of treasure) not aloof,
But with a famishing passion quick to grab
Meaning, and read on all the leaves of sin
Eternity's secret script, the saving proof.

EFFIGIES

I

His glances were directive, seemed to move
Pawns on a secret chess-board. You could fancy
You saw the pieces in their wooden dance
Leap in geometrical obedience
From square to square, or stop like broken clockwork
When silence spoke its checkmate. Past that arena
Stretched out a winding moonlight labyrinth,
A shining limbo filled with vanishing faces,

Propitious or dangerous, to be scanned
In a passion of repulsion or desire.
His glances knew two syllables: 'Come' and 'Go'.
When he was old and dull his eyes grew weary,
Gazing so long into the shifting maze,
And narrowed to the semi-circle before him,
The last defence. There if a stranger entered,
His heart, that beat regardless far within,
Grew still, a hawk before the deadly drop,
Then beat again as his quick mind found the gambit.
All this he hardly knew. His face was like
The shining front of a rich and loveless house,
The doors all shut. The windows cast such brightness
Outwards that none could see what was within,
Half-blinded by the strong repelling dazzle.
Set in the doors two little judas windows
Sometimes would catch the timid visitor's eye
And he would grow aware of a nameless something,
Animal or human, watching his approach,
Like darkness out of darkness. When he was dying
The pieces sauntered freely about the board
Like lawless vagrants, and would not be controlled.
He would whisper 'Stop,'
Starting awake, and weep to think they were free.

2

Pity the poor betrayer in the maze
That closed about him when he set the trap
To catch his friend. Now he is there alone,
The envied and beloved quarry fled
Long since for death and freedom. And the maze
Is like an odd device to marvel at
With other eyes if other eyes could see it;
As curious as an idle prince's toy.

234

There he is now, lost in security,
Quite, quite inside, no fissure in the walls,
Nor any sign of the door that led him in;
Only the oblivious labyrinth all around.
He did not dream of the trap within the trap
In the mad moment, nor that he would long
Sometime to have the beloved victim there
For the deep winding dialogue without end.
Pity him, for he cannot think the thought
Nor feel the pang that yet might set him free,
And Judas ransomed dangle from the tree.

3

Revolving in his own
Immovable danger zone,
Having killed his enemy
And betrayed his troublesome friend
To be with himself alone,
He watched upon the floor
The punctual minutes crawl
Towards the remaining wall
Into eternity,
And thought, 'Here is the end.'
Cut off in blind desire,
From the window he would see,
Twisting in twisted glass,
The devastated street,
The houses all gone wrong,
Watch hats and hurrying feet,
Wild birds and horses pass,
Think, 'All shall go up in fire,
Horse, man and city, all.'
Or dream a whole day long
Of miles and miles of way

Through hills down to the sea
At peace in a distant day;
Gazing upon the floor.
No knock upon the door.

4

We fired and fired, and yet they would not fall,
But stood on the ridge and bled,
Transfixed against the sky as on a wall,
Though they and we knew they were dead.
Then we went on,
Passed through them or between;
But all our eyes could fasten upon
Was a great broken machine,
Or so it seemed. Then on the ridge ahead
We watched them rise again.
I do not think we knew the dead
Were real, or really dead, till then.

5

She lived in comfort on her poor few pence
And sweetly starved to feed her swelling dream
Where all she had done came back in grievous blessing.
She had left her house and was by her lover left,
Her flying wings struck root upon his shoulders,
And in the self-same flight bore him away.
Her life was all an aria and an echo,
And when the aria ceased the echo led her
Gently to alight somewhere that seemed the earth.
There gradually she withered towards her harvest,
That grew as she grew less, until at last
She stared in grief at mounds and mounds of grain.

THE DIFFICULT LAND

This is a difficult land. Here things miscarry
Whether we care, or do not care enough.
The grain may pine, the harlot weed grow haughty,
Sun, rain, and frost alike conspire against us:
You'd think there was malice in the very air.
And the spring floods and summer droughts: our fields
Mile after mile of soft and useless dust.
On dull delusive days presaging rain
We yoke the oxen, go out harrowing,
Walk in the middle of an ochre cloud,
Dust rising before us and falling again behind us,
Slowly and gently settling where it lay.
These days the earth itself looks sad and senseless.
And when next day the sun mounts hot and lusty
We shake our fists and kick the ground in anger.
We have strange dreams: as that, in the early morning
We stand and watch the silver drift of stars
Turn suddenly to a flock of black-birds flying.
And once in a lifetime men from over the border,
In early summer, the season of fresh campaigns,
Come trampling down the corn, and kill our cattle.
These things we know and by good luck or guidance
Either frustrate or, if we must, endure.
We are a people; race and speech support us,
Ancestral rite and custom, roof and tree,
Our songs that tell of our triumphs and disasters
(Fleeting alike), continuance of fold and hearth,
Our names and callings, work and rest and sleep,
And something that, defeated, still endures—
These things sustain us. Yet there are times
When name, identity, and our very hands,
Senselessly labouring, grow most hateful to us,
And we would gladly rid us of these burdens,

Enter our darkness through the doors of wheat
And the light veil of grass (leaving behind
Name, body, country, speech, vocation, faith)
And gather into the secrecy of the earth
Furrowed by broken ploughs lost deep in time.

We have such hours, but are drawn back again
By faces of goodness, faithful masks of sorrow,
Honesty, kindness, courage, fidelity,
The love that lasts a life's time. And the fields,
Homestead and stall and barn, springtime and autumn.
(For we can love even the wandering seasons
In their inhuman circuit.) And the dead
Who lodge in us so strangely, unremembered,
Yet in their place. For how can we reject
The long last look on the ever-dying face
Turned backward from the other side of time?
And how offend the dead and shame the living
By these despairs? And how refrain from love?
This is a difficult country, and our home.

NOTHING THERE BUT FAITH

Nothing, it seemed, between them and the grave.
No, as I looked, there was nothing anywhere.
You'd think no ground could be so flat and bare:
No little ridge or hump or bush to brave
The horizon. Yet they called that land their land,
Without a single thought drank in that air
As simple and equivocal as despair.
This, this was what I could not understand.

238

The reason was, there was nothing there but faith.
Faith made the whole, yes all they could see or hear
Or touch or think, and arched its break of day
Within them and around them every way.
They looked: all was transfigured far and near,
And the great world rolled between them and death.

DOUBLE ABSENCE

The rust-red moon above the rose-red cloud,
Ethereal gifts of the absconding sun
That now is shining full on other lands
And soon will draw its track a hundred miles
Across the quiet breast of the hushed Atlantic.
The smoke grows up, solid, an ashen tree
From the high Abbey chimney. A sycamore
Holds on its topmost tip a singing thrush,
Its breast turned towards the sign of the buried sun.
Chance only brings such rare felicities
Beyond contrivance of the adventuring mind,
Strange past all meaning, set in their place alone.
Now the moon rises clear and fever pale
Out from the cloud's dissolving drift of ashes,
While in my mind, in double absence, hangs
The rust-red moon above the rose-red cloud.

DAY AND NIGHT

I wrap the blanket of the night
About me, fold on fold on fold—
And remember how as a child
Lost in the newness of the light

I first discovered what is old
From the night and the soft night wind.
For in the daytime all was new,
Moving in light and in the mind
All at once, thought, shape and hue.
Extravagant novelty too wild
For the new eyes of a child.

The night, the night alone is old
And showed me only what I knew,
Knew, yet never had been told;
A speech that from the darkness grew
Too deep for daily tongues to say,
Archaic dialogue of a few
Upon the sixth or the seventh day.
And shapes too simple for a place
In the day's shrill complexity
Came and were more natural, more
Expected than my father's face
Smiling across the open door,
More simple than the sanded floor
In unexplained simplicity.

A man now, gone with time so long—
My youth to myself grown fabulous
As an old land's memories, a song
To trouble or to pleasure us—
I try to fit that world to this,
The hidden to the visible play,
Would have them both, would nothing miss,
Learn from the shepherd of the dark,
Here in the light, the paths to know
That thread the labyrinthine park,
And the great Roman roads that go
Striding across the untrodden day.

THE OTHER STORY

How for the new thing can there be a word?
How can we know
The act, the form itself, unnamed, unheard,
Or for the first time go
Again on the road that runs ere memory
Snares it in syllables
And rings its burial bells
In gossip or music or poetry?
Yet we would not remember, but would be.

Why should we muse
On this great world that always is no more,
Or hope to hear sometime the great lost news?
It was all before.
And we would be where we were bred,
In Eden an hour away,
Though still our cheeks are red
For what is only in remembrance
Revolt or sin or guilt or shame,
Or some word much the same,
But was a haze of blood from foot to head,
Was that, and nothing said.
Innocent, knowing nothing of innocence,
We learned it from the sad memorial name
First uttered by the offence.
And now the two words seem
A single, fabulous, reciprocal glory,
A dream re-enacted in another dream,
And all accomplished as we plucked the bough.

Stories we know. There is another story.
If one of you is innocent let him tell it now.

DREAM AND THING

This is the thing, this truly is the thing.
We dreamt it once; now it has come about.
That was the dream, but this, this is the thing.
The dream was bold and thought it could foretell
What time would bring, but time, it seems, can bring
Only this thing which never has had a doubt
That everything is much like everything,
And the deep family likeness will come out.
We thought the dream would spread its folded wing;
But here's a thing that's neither sick nor well,
Stupid nor wise, and has no story to tell,
Though every tale is about it and about.
That is the thing, that is the very thing.
Yet take another look and you may bring
From the dull mass each separate splendour out.
There is no trust but in the miracle.

SONG FOR A HYPOTHETICAL AGE

Grief, they say, is personal,
Else there'd be no grief at all.
We, exempt from grief and rage,
Rule here our new impersonal age.
Now while dry is every eye
The last grief is passing by.
History takes its final turn
Where all's to mourn for, none to mourn.
Idle justice sits alone
In a world to order grown.
Justice never shed a tear,

242

And if justice we would bear
We must get another face,
Find a smoother tale to tell
Where everything is in its place
And happiness inevitable.

(Long, long ago, the old men say,
A famous wife, Penelope,
For twenty years the pride of Greece,
Wove and unwove a web all day
That might have been a masterpiece—
If she had let it have its way—
To drive all artistry to despair
And set the sober world at play
Beyond the other side of care,
And lead a fabulous era in.
But still she said, 'Where I begin
Must I return, else all is lost,
And great Odysseus tempest-tossed
Will perish, shipwrecked on my art.
But so, I guide him to the shore.'
And again the web she tore,
No more divided from her heart.)

Oh here the hot heart petrifies
And the round earth to rock is grown
In the winter of our eyes;
Heart and earth a single stone.
Until the stony barrier break
Grief and joy no more shall wake.

THE YOUNG PRINCES

There was a time: we were young princelings then
In artless state, with brows as bright and clear
As morning light on a new morning land.
We gave and took with innocent hands, not knowing
If we were rich or poor, or thinking at all
Of yours or mine; we were newcomers still,
And to have asked the use of that or this,
Its price, commodity, profit would have been
Discourtesy to it and shame to us.
We saw the earth stretched out to us in welcome,
But in our hearts we were the welcomers,
And so were courteous to all that was
In high simplicity and natural pride
To be so hailed and greeted with such glory
(Like absentminded kings who are proffered all
And need not have a penny in their pockets).
And when the elders told the ancestral stories,
Even as they spoke we knew the characters,
The good and bad, the simple and sly, the heroes,
Each in his place, and chance that turns the tale
To grief or joy; we saw and accepted all.
Then in the irreversible noonday came,
Showering its darts into our open breasts,
Doubt that kills courtesy and gratitude.
Since then we have led our dull discourteous lives,
Heaven doubting and earth doubting. Earth and heaven
Bent to our menial use. And yet sometimes
We still, as through a dream that comes and goes,
Know what we are, remembering what we were.

THE CLOUD

One late spring evening in Bohemia,
Driving to the Writers' House, we lost our way
In a maze of little winding roads that led
To nothing but themselves,
Weaving a rustic web for thoughtless travellers.
No house was near, nor sign or sound of life:
Only a chequer-board of little fields,
Crumpled and dry, neat squares of powdered dust.
At a sudden turn we saw
A young man harrowing, hidden in dust; he seemed
A prisoner walking in a moving cloud
Made by himself for his own purposes;
And there he grew and was as if exalted
To more than man, yet not, not glorified:
A pillar of dust moving in dust; no more.
The bushes by the roadside were encrusted
With a hard sheath of dust.
We looked and wondered; the dry cloud moved on
With its interior image.
                              Presently we found
A road that brought us to the Writers' House,
And there a preacher from Urania
(Sad land where hope each day is killed by hope)
Praised the good dust, man's ultimate salvation,
And cried that God was dead. As we drove back
Late to the city, still our minds were teased
By the brown barren fields, the harrowing,
The figure walking in its cloud, the message
From far Urania. This was before the change;
And in our memory cloud and message fused,
Image and thought condensed to a giant form
That walked the earth clothed in its earthly cloud,
Dust made sublime in dust. And yet it seemed unreal

And lonely as things not in their proper place.
And thinking of the man
Hid in his cloud we longed for light to break
And show that his face was the face once broken in Eden
Beloved, world-without-end lamented face;
And not a blindfold mask on a pillar of dust.

THE HORSES

Barely a twelvemonth after
The seven days war that put the world to sleep,
Late in the evening the strange horses came.
By then we had made our covenant with silence,
But in the first few days it was so still
We listened to our breathing and were afraid.
On the second day
The radios failed; we turned the knobs; no answer.
On the third day a warship passed us, heading north,
Dead bodies piled on the deck. On the sixth day
A plane plunged over us into the sea. Thereafter
Nothing. The radios dumb;
And still they stand in corners of our kitchens,
And stand, perhaps, turned on, in a million rooms
All over the world. But now if they should speak,
If on a sudden they should speak again,
If on the stroke of noon a voice should speak,
We would not listen, we would not let it bring
That old bad world that swallowed its children quick
At one great gulp. We would not have it again.
Sometimes we think of the nations lying asleep,
Curled blindly in impenetrable sorrow,
And then the thought confounds us with its strangeness.

The tractors lie about our fields; at evening
They look like dank sea-monsters couched and waiting.
We leave them where they are and let them rust:
'They'll moulder away and be like other loam'.
We make our oxen drag our rusty ploughs,
Long laid aside. We have gone back
Far past our fathers' land.
                              And then, that evening
Late in the summer the strange horses came.
We heard a distant tapping on the road,
A deepening drumming; it stopped, went on again
And at the corner changed to hollow thunder.
We saw the heads
Like a wild wave charging and were afraid.
We had sold our horses in our fathers' time
To buy new tractors. Now they were strange to us
As fabulous steeds set on an ancient shield
Or illustrations in a book of knights.
We did not dare go near them. Yet they waited,
Stubborn and shy, as if they had been sent
By an old command to find our whereabouts
And that long-lost archaic companionship.
In the first moment we had never a thought
That they were creatures to be owned and used.
Among them were some half-a-dozen colts
Dropped in some wilderness of the broken world,
Yet new as if they had come from their own Eden.
Since then they have pulled our ploughs and borne our loads,
But that free servitude still can pierce our hearts.
Our life is changed; their coming our beginning.

SONG

This will not pass so soon,
Dear friend, this will not pass,
Though time is out of tune
With all beneath the moon,
Man and woman and flower and grass.
These will not pass.
For there's a word 'Return'
That's known among the quick and the dead,
Making two realms for ever cry and mourn.
So mourns the land of darkness when
Into the light away the lily is led,
And so gives thanks again
When from the earth the snow-pale beauty goes
Back to her home. Persephone,
Surely all this can only be
A light exchange and amorous interplay
In your strange twofold immortality;
And a diversion for a summer day
The death and resurrection of the rose.

THE ISLAND

Your arms will clasp the gathered grain
For your good time, and wield the flail
In merry fire and summer hail.
There stand the golden hills of corn
Which all the heroic clans have borne,
And bear the herdsmen of the plain,
The horseman in the mountain pass,
The archaic goat with silver horn,
Man, dog and flock and fruitful hearth.

Harvests of men to men give birth.
These the ancestral faces bred
And show as through a golden glass
Dances and temples of the dead.
Here speak through the transmuted tongue
The full grape bursting in the press,
The barley seething in the vat,
Which earth and man as one confess,
Babbling of what both would be at
In garrulous story and drunken song.
Though come a different destiny,
Though fall a universal wrong
More stern than simple savagery,
Men are made of what is made,
The meat, the drink, the life, the corn,
Laid up by them, in them reborn.
And self-begotten cycles close
About our way; indigenous art
And simple spells make unafraid
The haunted labyrinths of the heart,
And with our wild succession braid
The resurrection of the rose.

Sicily

INTO THIRTY CENTURIES BORN

Into thirty centuries born,
At home in them all but the very last,
We meet ourselves at every turn
In the long country of the past.
There the fallen are up again
In mortality's second day,

There the indisputable dead
Rise in flesh more fine than clay
And the dead selves we cast away
In imperfection are perfected,
And all is plain yet never found out!
Ilium burns before our eyes
For thirty centuries never put out,
And we walk the streets of Troy
And breathe in the air its fabulous name.
The king, the courtier and the rout
Shall never perish in that flame;
Old Priam shall become a boy
For ever changed, for ever the same.

What various sights these countries show:
The horses on the roundabout
Still flying round the glittering ring
That rusted fifty years ago.
The gunboat in the little bay,
A mile, and half an age away.
Methuselah letting the years go by
While death was new and still in doubt
And only a dream the thought, 'To die'.
And round a corner you may see
Man, maid and tempter under the tree:
You'd think there was no sense in death.
And nothing to remedy, nothing to blame;
The dark Enchanter is your friend.
Is it fantasy or faith
That keeps intact that marvellous show
And saves the helpless dead from harm?—
To-morrow sounds the great alarm
That puts the histories to rout;
To-morrow after to-morrow brings
Endless beginning without end.

Then on this moment set your foot,
Take your road for everywhere,
And from your roving barrier shoot
Your arrow into the empty air.
Follow at a careful pace,
Else you may wander in despair.
Gathered at your moving post
Is all that you have but memory.
This is the place of hope and fear,
And faith that comes when hope is lost.
Defeat and victory both are here.
In this place where all's to be,
In this moment you are free,
And bound to all. For you shall know
Before you Troy goes up in fire,
And you shall walk the Trojan streets
When home are sailed the murdering fleets,
Priam shall be a little boy,
Time shall cancel time's deceits,
And you shall weep for grief and joy
To see the whole world perishing
Into everlasting spring,
And over and over the opening briar.

MY OWN

There's nothing here to keep me from my own.—
The confident roads that at their ease beguile me
With the all-promising lands, the great unknown,
Can with their gilded dust blind me, defile me.
It's so. Yet never did their lies deceive me,
And when, lost in the dreaming route, I say
I seek my soul, my soul does not believe me,
But from these transports turns displeased away.

But then, but then, why should I so behave me,
Willingly duped ten, twenty times an hour,
But that even at my dearest cost I'd save me
From the true knowledge and the real power?
In which through all time's changeable seasons grown,
I might have stayed, unshaken, with my own.

IF I COULD KNOW

If I could truly know that I do know
This, and the foreshower of this show,
Who is myself, for plot and scene are mine,
They say, and the world my sign,
Man, earth and heaven, co-patterned so or so—
If I could know.

If I could swear that I do truly see
The real world, and all itself and free,
Not prisoned in my shallow sight's confine,
Nor mine, but to be mine,
Freely sometime to come and be with me—
If I could see.

If I could tell that I do truly hear
A music, not this tumult in my ear
Of all that cries in the world, confused or fine;
If there were staff and sign
Pitched high above the battle of hope and fear—
If I could hear.

Make me to see and hear that I may know
This journey and the place towards which I go;
For a beginning and an end are mine
Surely, and have their sign
Which I and all in the earth and the heavens show.
Teach me to know.

THE LATE WASP

You that through all the dying summer
Came every morning to our breakfast table,
A lonely bachelor mummer,
And fed on the marmalade
So deeply, all your strength was scarcely able
To prise you from the sweet pit you had made,—
You and the earth have now grown older,
And your blue thoroughfares have felt a change;
They have grown colder;
And it is strange
How the familiar avenues of the air
Crumble now, crumble; the good air will not hold,
All cracked and perished with the cold;
And down you dive through nothing and through despair.

THE LATE SWALLOW

Leave, leave your well-loved nest,
Late swallow, and fly away.
Here is no rest
For hollowing heart and wearying wing.
Your comrades all have flown
To seek their southern paradise
Across the great earth's downward sloping side,
And you are alone.
Why should you cling
Still to the swiftly ageing narrowing day?
Prepare;
Shake out your pinions long untried
That now must bear you there where you would be
Through all the heavens of ice;
Till falling down the homing air
You light and perch upon the radiant tree.

SONG

This that I give and take,
This that I keep and break,
Is and is not my own
But lives in itself alone,
Yet is between us two,
Mine only in the breaking,
It all in the remaking,
Doing what I undo.

With it all must be well,
There where the invisible
Loom sweetly plies its trade.
All made there is well-made.
So be it between us two;
A giving be our taking,
A making our unmaking,
A doing what we undo.

Poems Not Previously Collected

*

(See Note on page 7)

I

SONNET

You will not leave us, for You cannot, Lord.
We are the inventors of disloyalty,
And every day proclaim we dare not be
Ourselves' or Yours: at every point absurd.
For this was forged the counterfeiting word
By which the hours beguile eternity
Or cry that You are dead Who cannot die.
So in a word You are glorified and abjured.

Yet say You died and left where once You were
Nothing at all—man, beast and plant as now
In semblance, yet mere obvious nature—how
Could the blind paradox, the ridiculous
Find entrance then? What would remain with us?
Nothing, nothing at all, not even despair.

THE SONG

I was haunted all that day by memories knocking
At a disused, deaf, dead door of my mind
Sealed up for forty years by myself and time.
They could not get to me nor I to them.
And yet they knocked. And since I could not answer,
Since time was past for that sole assignation,
I was oppressed by the unspoken thought
That they and I were not contemporary,
For I had gone away. Yet still in dreams
Where all is changed, time, place, identity,

Where fables turn to beasts and beasts to fables,
And anything can be in a natural wonder,
These meetings are renewed, dead dialogues
Utter their antique speech.
                              That night I dreamed
That towards the end of such another day
Spent in such thoughts, but in some other place,
I was returning from a long day's work—
What work I have forgotten—and had to cross
A park lost somewhere in the world, yet now
Present and whole to me as I to it:
Utilitarian strip of grass and trees—
A short-cut for poor clerks to unhallowed rooms.
I stopped beside the gate—as how often before?—
When from the park poured out the resonant moaning
Of some great beast in anguish. Could it be
For us, I wondered dreaming, the strange beast mourned,
Or for some deed once done and done for ever
And done in vain?
                    And yet I pushed the gate—
As how often before?—passed through and went my way,
When on my right appeared what seemed a cliff
Newly arisen there beside the path.
Was this the park, I thought, or had I strayed
Into some place forgotten in old time?
The dream worked on; I looked again and saw
The huge hind-quarters of some giant thing;
A horse it seemed that first had been a cliff.
As heavy as earth it stood and mourned alone,
Horse, or centaur, or wide-winged Pegasus,
But far too strange for any fabulous name.
I thought, here is no place for pity, I cannot share
That sorrow whose only speech is dread and awe.
And then in terror lest the thing should move
And come on me, I ran to the farther gate,

Stood there and listened. Darkness had fallen,
But still that wonder
Sent out its moan not meant for other ears,
A long breath drawn by pain, intolerable.

I thought, now it will move. And then it moved.
The moaning ceased, the hoofs rose up and fell
Gently, as treading out a meditation,
Then broke in thunder; the wild thing charged the gate,
Yet could not pass—oh pity!—that simple barrier
(Subservient to any common touch),
Turned back again in absolute overthrow,
And beat on the ground as if for entrance there.
The dream worked on. The clamour died; the hoofs
Beat on no common ground; silence; a drumming
As of wild swans taking their highway south
From the murdering ice; hoofs, wings far overhead
Climbing the sky; pain raised that wonder there;
Nothing but pain. The drumming died away.

Was it these hoofs, I thought, that knocked all day
With no articulate message, but this vision
That had no tongue to speak its mystery?
What wound in the world's side and we unknowing
Lay open and bleeding now? What present anguish
Drew that long dirge from the earth-haunting marvel?
And why that earthly visit, unearthly pain?
I was not dreaming now, but thinking the dream.
Then all was quiet, the park was its own again,
And I on my road to my familiar lodgings
A world away; and all its poor own again.
Yet I woke up saying, 'The song—the song'.

IMAGES

I

Take one look at that face and go your way.
Regard these lines of motionless desire
Perpetually assuaged yet unappeased,
Still yearning for what still is about to be.
What you see there is something else than beauty.
These are your lineaments, the face of life
When it is quite alone, and you forgotten.
Look once. But do not hope to find a sentence
To tell what you have seen. Stop at the colon:
And set a silence after to speak the word
That you will always seek and never find,
Perhaps, if found, the good and beautiful end.
You will not reach that place. So leave the hiatus
There in the broken sentence. What is missing
You will always think of. And do not turn again
To scan that face lest you should leave upon it
Your personal load of trouble and desire.
You cannot add to it nor take away.
All that you think or say will be a postscript
To that imperfect mystery, limping sentence.
And do not forget. But look once at that face.

II

You in imaginary fears
Threading the terrors of a wood
That has no place but in your mind;
You hunted by the ravenous years
That send their warnings through your blood
Where fears long conquered still affright;
You willingly gone to be with blind

Tiresias in his buried night
That opens at an idle word—
You look in wonder at the bird,
Round ball of appetite and fear,
That sings at ease upon the branch,
Time a long silence in its ear
That never heard of time or space;
You who hear the avalanche
Must fabricate a temporal tale
To bring the timeless nightingale
And swallow to your trysting place.

III

He is the little, sly, absconding god,
Hides in the moment. Look, and he is gone,
But turn away, and there he is back again.
He is more quick than movement,
Present and gone, absent and safe in hiding,
No spell can bind him. But idle fools and children
Take him for granted, are at their ease with him,
And he's the true friend of the absentminded.
He is too agile for time's dull iambics,
Lightly dives in and out of stale duration,
Poised on the endless present. There he is free,
Having no past or future. All things know him.
And then are eased as by a heavenly chance.
The greater gods sometimes in grave amusement
Smile at his tricks, yet nod in approbation.

COMPLAINT OF THE DYING PEASANTRY

Our old songs are lost,
Our sons are newspapermen
At the singers' cost.
There were no papers when

Sir Patrick Spens put out to sea
In all the country cottages
With music and ceremony
For five centuries.

Till Scott and Hogg, the robbers, came
And nailed the singing tragedies down
In dumb letters under a name
And led the bothy to the town.

Sir Patrick Spens shut in a book,
Burd Helen stretched across a page:
A few readers look
There at the effigy of our age.

The singing and the harping fled
Into the silent library;
But we are with Helen dead
And with Sir Patrick lost at sea.

THE CHURCH

This autumn day the new cross is set up
On the unfinished church, above the trees,
Bright as a new penny, tipping the tip
Of the elongated spire in the sunny breeze,
And is at ease;
Newcomer suddenly, calmly looking down
On this American university town.

Someone inside me sketches a cross—askew,
A child's—on seeing that stick crossed with a stick,
Some simple ancestor, perhaps, that knew,
Centuries ago when all were Catholic,
That this archaic trick
Brings to the heart and the fingers what was done
One spring day in Judaea to Three in One;

When God and Man in more than love's embrace,
Far from their heaven and tumult died,
And the holy Dove fluttered above that place
Seeking its desolate nest in the broken side,
And Nature cried
To see Heaven doff its glory to atone
For man, lest he should die in time, alone.

I think of the Church, that stretched magnificence
Housing the crib, the desert, and the tree,
And the good Lord who lived on poverty's pence
Among the fishermen of Galilee,
Courting mortality,
And schooled himself to learn his human part:
A poor man skilled in dialectic art.

What reason for that splendour of blue and gold
For One so great and poor He was past all need?
What but impetuous love that could not hold
Its storm of spending and must scatter its seed
In blue and gold and deed,
And write its busy Books on Books of Days
To attempt and never touch the sum of praise.

I look at the church again, and yet again,
And think of those who house together in Hell,
Cooped by ingenious theological men
Expert to track the sour and musty smell

Of sins they know too well;
Until grown proud, they crib in rusty bars
The Love that moves the sun and the other stars.

Yet fortune to the new church, and may its door
Never be shut, or yawn in empty state
To daunt the poor in spirit, the always poor.
Catholic, Orthodox, Protestant, may it wait
Here for its true estate.
All's still to do; roof, window and wall are bare.
I look, and do not doubt that He is there.

SALEM, MASSACHUSETTS

They walked black Bible streets and piously tilled
The burning fields of the new Apocalypse.
With texts and guns they drove the Indians out,
Ruled young and old with stiff Hebraic rod,
The Puritan English country gentlemen;
And burned young witches.
                              Their sons' grandsons
Throve on Leviathan and the China trade
And built and lived in beautiful wooden houses,
Their Jordan past.
                         You may see the Witches' Trail
Still winding through the streets to a little knoll
That looks across a tideless inland bay
In the clear New England weather. This they saw,
The women, till the fire and smoke consumed
Sight, breath and body while the Elders watched
That all was well and truly consumed by fire.
The House with the Seven Gables is gone, consumed by fire,
And in the evenings businessmen from Boston
Sit in the beautiful houses, mobbed by cars.

AFTER A HYPOTHETICAL WAR

No rule nor ruler: only water and clay,
And the purblind peasant squatting, elbows out
To nudge his neighbour from his inch of ground
Clutched fast through flood and drought but never loved.
Avarice without meaning. There you will see
The soil on its perpetual death-bed; miles
Of mendicant flowers prospering on its bier,
And weeds as old as time, their roots entangled,
Murderer choking murderer in the dark,
Though here they rule and flourish. Heaven and earth
Give only of their worst, breeding what's bad.
Even the dust-cart meteors on their rounds
Stop here to void their refuse, leaving this
Chaotic breed of misbegotten things,
Embryos of what could never wish to be.
Soil and air breed crookedly here, and men
Are dumb and twisted as the envious scrub
That spreads in silent malice on the fields.
Lost lands infected by an enmity
Deeper than lust or greed, that works by stealth
Yet in the sun is helpless as the blindworm,
Making bad worse. The mud has sucked half in
People and cattle until they eat and breathe
Nothing but mud. Poor tribe so meanly cheated,
Their very cradle an image of the grave.
What rule or governance can save them now?

THE CONQUEROR

But oh that rich encrimsoned cloud
From which rode out the armoured man.
He saw his kingdom stretched below
And thought that he need scarcely go
To take it, his ere he began.
You well might think that he was proud.

We waited for the advent. Then
Some hesitation held him there.
Was it the little roads that made
The simple conqueror afraid?
Defeat came on him in the air,
And the soft cloud drank him in again.

AN ISLAND TALE

She had endured so long a grief
That from her breast we saw it grow,
Branch, leaf and flower with such a grace
We wondered at the summer place
Which set that harvest there. But oh
The softly, softly yellowing leaf.

She was enclosed in quietness,
Where for lost love her tears were shed.
They stopped, and she was quite alone.
Being so poor, she was our own,
Her lack of all our precious bread.
She had no skill to offer less.

She turned into an island song
And died. They sing her ballad yet,
But all the simple verses tell
Is, Love and grief became her well.
Too well; for how can we forget
Her happy face when she was young?

AFTER 1984

Even now we speak of Eighty-four
Although that world is far away.
It is not strange that children play
Their games again. . . . A random score
Of veterans still recall the day
That drove the murdering lies away.

The young say that necessity
Decided all should happen so;
Men did not act, but history.—
We who remember do not know,
And still to us the event is strange.
We cannot understand that change.

For how from nothing could come so much?
We the deprived and uncommitted,
Nothing being left us to commit,
Who could not even be manumitted
Because no one could see or touch
Our fetters locked so far within,
And not a key in the world to fit;
We who had been so carefully bred
Not to feel sorrow or be pleased—
How could we ever be released?

Turn about widdershins and be free?
Love and murder, pity and sin
Turned our monotone to red.

The secret universe of the blind
Cannot be known. Just so we were
Shut from ourselves even in our mind;
Only a twisting chaos within
Turned on itself, not knowing where
The exit was, salvation gate.
Was it chaos that set us straight,
The elements that rebelled, not we?
Or the anguish never to find
Ourselves, somewhere, at last, and be?
We must escape, no matter where.

Accident? Miracle? Then we fought
On to this life that was before,
Only that, no less, no more,
Strangely familiar. In the Nought
Did we beget it in our thought?

THE STRANGE RETURN

Behind him Hell sank in the plain.
He saw far off the liquid glaze
Of burning somewhere. That was all.
A burning there or in his brain?
He could not tell. His was a case,
He thought, that put all Hell in doubt,
Though he had cause to know that place.
Had They some darker thought in mind,

Arranged his flight, inveigled him out
To walk half-way from Heaven to Hell?
Was where he stood a dream of stone?
No matter, he was here alone.
And then he saw the tangled skein,
His foot-prints following him behind
And stretching to the prison lock,
And there two towers like ears a-cock.
Would they answer to his knock,
Brush all aside, invite him in,
Crack a dry witticism on sin,
Excuse his saunter over the sand,
If he returned? Or understand?
But then the towers like ears a-cock.

How from that bastion could he fall
Like Lazarus backwards into life
And travel to another death?
And now in buried distances
There was a wakening and he heard
Word at odds with common word,
A child's voice crying, "Let me be!"
In a world he could not touch,
And others saying, "Be in time",
With such a strange anxiety
(And he himself caught here in time).
The young girl's brow, the vertical cleft
Above the eyes that saw too much
Too soon: how could he counter these,
Make friends with the evils, take his part,
Salute the outer and inner strife,
The bickering between doubt and faith,
Inherit the tangle he had left,
Outface the trembling at his heart?

Three feet away a little tree
Put out in pain a single bud
That did not fear the ultimate fire.
And in a flash he knew it all,
The long-forgotten and new desire,
And looked and saw the tree was good.

THREE TALES

See, they move past, linked wrist to wrist with time,
Wise man and fool, straggler and good recruit,
Enlisted in the enigma's exploration.
They cannot read its purpose, only guess
There is no turning back, no deviation,
Nor resting place on the enormous road.
There are three tales of time. The first one says
The traveller in his mind created it
That there might be a theme, a great flawed story
To interrupt the unbearable trance of peace,
And for that gain time was a trifling fee.
The second holds that time was there already
Before we came, and that our opening eyes
Struck full upon it. This, they say, is why
We know the changing world, for all was there
In that first look, with no division.
The rest was Afterwards. The third tale says
That we were born into eternity,
The boundless garden, and our issuing thence
Was self-incarceration in a prison
Where we act out our wishes' wild succession.
The crystal walls are scrawled with static signs,
But as we advance our towering shadows move
With our own motion, melting in multitude.

So we go forward linked with numberless shadow,
Invisible, inaudible close companion,
Dear friend and enemy in our flight from time.

THE DESOLATIONS

The desolations are not the sorrows' kin.
Sorrow is gentle and sings her sons to rest.
The desolations have no word nor music,
Only an endless inarticulate cry
Inaudible to the poetry-pampered ear.
The desolations tell
Nothing for ever, the interminable
Civil war of earth and water and fire.
These have to do with our making.
                              What guards us here
Among the established and familiar things?
The leaf, the apple and the rounded earth
Where even imagination is an O,
And only endless harvest is gathered there,
Nothing but that. Yet sometimes absently
We pause and murmur "We came crying hither",
Remembering, and set up a little stage
For our indigenous formal tragedy
Where we are all the actors.
                              The wild earth
Pours its hot entrails on the slopes of Aetna,
Blasting whatever's made. Yet in a while
Black house-rows like a pleasant street in Hell
Rise from the frozen slag, and safe within
The lava rooms Sicilian families
Follow their ancient ways; the vine-rows yield
Seven times a year, fed on earth's dearest dust.

And all forget the admonition of fire.
There, if you listen, you may hear them say,
"Love is at home, earth's joys lie all around us,
The vine-stock and the rose are guarded well.
The roof-tree holds, and friends come in the evening."
What saves us from the raging desolations
And tells us we shall walk through peace to peace?

THE BROTHERS

Last night I watched my brothers play,
The gentle and the reckless one,
In a field two yards away.
For half a century they were gone
Beyond the other side of care
To be among the peaceful dead.
Even in a dream how could I dare
Interrogate that happiness
So wildly spent yet never less?
For still they raced about the green
And were like two revolving suns;
A brightness poured from head to head,
So strong I could not see their eyes
Or look into their paradise.
What were they doing, the happy ones?
Yet where I was they once had been.

I thought, How could I be so dull,
Twenty thousand days ago,
Not to see they were beautiful?
I asked them, Were you really so
As you are now, that other day?
And the dream was soon away.

For then we played for victory
And not to make each other glad.
A darkness covered every head,
Frowns twisted the original face,
And through that mask we could not see
The beauty and the buried grace.

I have observed in foolish awe
The dateless mid-days of the law
And seen indifferent justice done
By everyone on everyone.
And in a vision I have seen
My brothers playing on the green.

DIALOGUE

Returning from the antipodes of time,
What did you find, adventurer seeking your home?
What were you doing there in the dragon's kingdom?
Did you see yourself when you were not looking,
Or take the desert lion by surprise,
Entering his gaze following the antelope
To the watering place, watching the watcher, still
So far away from the unreachable beginning,
A soul seeking its soul in fell and claw?
Did you plunge in the smothering waters to peruse
In shell and glaucous eye your dateless scripture,
Or scan the desert with the desert's eyes,
Watching the sand-storm racing round the plain
On the vacant trace like a pack of spectral hounds?

273

Did they bring you comfort?
What were you doing there at the back of the world?

Returning now from the other side of time
My steps are measured and processional
In the archaic march led by the sun.
So it must be, the light leading, the foot
Stepping into the world in the opening moment.
Now, passing, I see that all is in its place,
The good and the evil, equal and strange order:
Hunter and quarry, each in a separate day,
The hecatombs of slaughter upon the hills,
The shepherds watching from the eastern slopes,
New gods and kings sitting upon their chairs
(I cannot read their faces),
War and peace, generation and death,
Shameful and sad concurrences of time,
The uncanny stillness of the savage keep,
The blackened gorge nothing can clean again
Where thirty thousand, men and women and children,
Were slaughtered once (no one will walk there now),
The hungry waste advancing and retiring,
Violent or invisible alteration,
The transmutations, child and youth and man,
Maiden and mother, maiden and mother again,
A man and a woman building their changing house
On patient mutability. And Jack and Jill
And Kate and Harry, black and brown and white,
Who keep the bond when faith and beauty leave,
And are there for their own and the world's good.
And the house-dog and the cat, timeless companions,
The bird that sang one day in the dragon's bower
And nests beneath my eaves, a little house-god,
The cattle in the meadow, and this my home.

But now, looking again, I see wall, roof and door
Are changed, and my house looks out on foreign ground.
This is not the end of the world's road.

Yet sometimes on an evening when all is still
And the bird in flight hangs tranced upon the air,
Flying and yet at rest, as if time's work were over,
And the sun burns red and still on the bole of the yew-tree,
And the workman, his day ended, stands and listens,
Thinking of home, yet held in the bright stillness,
I see you stand at your window and softly arrest
Tree, bird and man and the nightward hastening sun
In an endless stasis, and what was given before
You opened your eyes upon the changing earth
Is there, and for a moment you are at home.

That was a moment, now a memory.
I do not live in the house of memory.
For my kinsmen say: 'Long since we lost a road,
Then reached this place, on earth the first and last,
Neither good nor bad, the right place nor the wrong;
A house, and there we nourish a heavenly hope.
For this a great god died and all heaven mourned
That earth might, in extremity, have such fortune.
This we know. Yet in half-memory,
Not in complaint and scarcely in desire,
Sometimes we say: Long since we lost a road,
And feel the ghost of an ethereal sorrow
Passing, and lighting or darkening all the house,
Lighting or darkening, which, we do not know.
Does that road still run somewhere in the world?
Question on question.
Hope and sorrow ethereal roof our house.'

SICK CALIBAN

He looked, he saw, and quickly went his way.
Should he have cried
On all the world to help that suffering thing,
Man, beast, or bestial changeling,
Or huge fish stranded choking in dry air
Without the sense to die?
Yet that great emerald blazing on its finger,
The proud and sneaking malice in its eye
That said, I suffer truly and yet malinger,
Long for and hate the stupid remedy.
Look: I am yourself for ever stuck half way.

And then he knew
Those he would summon were a multiplied
Mere replica of himself, and all had thought
Long since, No remedy here or anywhere
For that poor bag of bone
And hank of hair.

So he went on
And for a while could hear behind his back
A trifling rumour, mere imagined moan,
At last nothing at all. Yet now the lack
Began to irk him and the silence grew
Into a dead weight shut within his side,
And he knew
That he must carry it now, be patient and wise
Until perhaps in the end time would devise
A meaning, a light and simple syllable wrought
By a chance breath.

And so he took the straight road to his death
In surly anger that was far from mourning.
Behind him followed hope and faith

Saying little. But something stood at that first turning
By itself, weeping. If he could keep his eyes
On that far distant mourner, would it save
Something? Would he find breath to call
To the others, and all be changed, that thing, and all?

PENELOPE IN DOUBT

Forgotten brooch and shrivelled scar,
Were these the only guarantee
This was Odysseus? Did she go
Through twenty years of drifting snow,
Whitening that head and hers, to be
Near as a wife, and yet so far?

The brooch came closer as he told—
Grown suddenly young—how he had lost
The wild doe and the raging hound
That battled in the golden round.
She listened, but what shook her most
Was that these creatures made her old.

Odysseus and that idle tale—
How many things in her had died
While hound and doe shut in the ring
Still fought somewhere in the world, a thing
So strange, her heart knocked on her side.
His eyes with time were bleached and pale.

A stranger, who had seen too much,
Been where she could not follow, sealed
In blank and smooth estranging snow
From head to foot. How could she know
What a brown scar said or concealed?
Yet now she trembled at his touch.

THE TOWER

This is the famous Babel Tower,
You'd think it had grown since yesterday.
We are the architects of that power;
Oh, that the clouds would bear it away.
When our morning stint is done
We watch the mannikin sentries stand
Shoulder to shoulder with the sun
(They are like tribesmen of the air)
And view the geometrical line
Of shadow cutting in two our land.
What have we fashioned but a sign?
This unending quarry strewn
With rough and smooth and wicked stone
To mount that gun aimed at the sky:
What have we made but an empty sign?
The archaic clouds pass slowly by.
What are our masters? Who are you there?
We scarcely see you. May there come
A great wind from a stormier star,
Blow tower and shadow to kingdom come.

This is the old men's story. Once
Voices were there, resounding words
Of an incomprehensible tongue
Fit for great heroes and great lords,
But never spoken anywhere.
And once a simple country song
Began and suddenly ended. Since
No message drops from the middle air
Except when a dead lord flutters down
Light as a frozen and mummied fly
From the perpendicular town.
(They have no license there to die.)

We cannot bear to scan that face,
Cover in haste the unchristened head,
Heap dust and rubble upon the place.
We too die. *So* look the dead
Whose breath stopped on a different star.
Who are they? We are what we are.

SONNET

Do not mourn still your generation's blood,
And face rubbed bare by reasonable fears,
And unintentional tears
That fall and are lost. Better to chew the cud
Of ignorant earlier days (Forgive us, time)
Before experience preached the certainty
That what will be will be,
Telling us that we shall commit our crime.

Past odds and ends sustain us. We can suck
Courage from buried bravery's dear downfall,
Learn from forgotten fools to chance our luck
And cut our losses, piously recall
Those who believed and did not understand,
And built in faith and folly in this ancient land.

THE VOICES

The lid flew off, and all the desolations,
As through a roaring poet's shameless throat,
Poured out their lamentations.
It seemed somewhere they were trying to take a vote
That in the hurry and din was never taken,

For not one wrong was shaken.
And all as stupid and sad
As a cashiered and spavined army of horse
Charging behind their false archaic neigh
At a fantastical force
Ten thousand miles or years away;
Or as a tribe who having lost their tongue
Could find no articulate word to say,
Having forgotten what was fresh and young:
All so debased by time it was almost mad.

We were assembled for some ceremony,
Compelled to this music, forced to hear.
But as we listened insidious memory,
The secret spy within the ear,
Whispered, 'This is your speech, this is the rune
You never read; this is your oldest tune.'
At which we cried, 'Push, push it back under the ground.
We will not listen. We
Will not endure that sound,'
And in the clamour could not hear a voice
That calmly said, 'Rejoice.'

IMPERSONAL CALAMITY

Respectable men have witnessed terrible things,
And rich and poor things extraordinary,
These murder-haunted years. Even so, even so,
Respectable men seem still respectable,
The ordinary no less ordinary,
For our inherited features cannot show
More than traditional grief and happiness
That rise from old and worn and simple springs.
How can an eye or brow

Disclose the gutted towns and the millions dead?
They have too slight an artistry.
Between us and the things that change us
A covenant long ago was set
And is prescriptive yet.
A single grief from man or God
Freely will let
Change in and bring a stern relief.
A son or daughter dead
Can bend the back or whiten the head,
Break and remould the heart,
Stiffen the face into a mask of grief.
It is an ancient art.
The impersonal calamities estrange us
From our own selves, send us abroad
In desolate thoughtlessness,
While far behind our hearts know what they know,
Yet cannot feel, nor ever express.

THE TWO SISTERS

Her beauty was so rare,
It wore her body down
With leading through the air
That marvel not her own.
At last to set it free
From enmity of change
And time's incontinence
To drink from beauty's bone,
Snatching her last defence,
She locked it in the sea.

The other, not content
That fault of hers should bring

Grief and mismanagement
To make an end of grace
And snap the slender ring,
Pulled death down on her head,
Completed destiny.
So each from her own place,
These ladies put to sea
To join the intrepid dead.

THE LAST WAR

I

No place at all for bravery in that war
Nor mark where one might make a stand,
Nor use for eye or hand
To discover and reach the enemy
Hidden in boundless air.
No way to attempt, to save
By our own death the young that they might die
Sometime a different death. The thought Again
That made a promise to mortality—
Gave pathos and distance, reason and rhyme—
Will walk a little before us to the grave
While we are still in time for a little time.

II

Or shall we think only of night and day
Vacantly visiting the vacant earth
And stare in hatred at the turncoat sun
That shines on glittering oes where thought of birth
Will never be—till birth will be a dream
Of a quaint custom in another place,
And we shall gaze in wonder face to face?

Or shall we picture bird and tree
Silently falling, and think of all the words
By which we forged earth, night and day
And ruled with such strange ease our work and play?
Now only the lexicon of a dream.
And we see our bodies buried in falling birds.

III

Shall we all die together?
Perhaps nothing at all will be but pain,
A choking and floundering, or gigantic stupor
Of a world-wide deserted hospital ward.
There will be strange good-byes, more strange than those
That once were spoken by terrified refugees,
Our harbingers: some of them lost in shipwreck,
Spilling salt angry tears in the salt waves,
Their lives waste-water sucked through a gaping hole,
Yet all the world around them; hope and fear.
We thought too idly of them, not knowing we
Might founder on common earth and choke in air,
Without one witness. Will great visions come,
And life lie clear at last as it says, Good-bye,
Good-bye, I have borne with you a little while?
Or shall we remember shameful things concealed,
Mean coldnesses and wounds too eagerly given?

IV

A tree thin sick and pale by a north wall,
A smile splintering a face—
I saw them today, suddenly made aware
That ordinary sights appal,

So that a tree mistreated wounds the heart,
A twisted smile twists inward through the mind
Ingeniously to find
Its place and claim a lifelong tenancy there.
That is not strange but the most ancient art,
I thought, consummate, still and blind.

I wondered if some pure ancestral head
Kept vigil there, but thought, Our eyes are led
Through endless circles of impure reflection,
Pilfering, pillaging what is not their own
In idle greed. Face mirrors face,
Mixing to generate an image sown
By casual desire or disaffection,
Assembles a common face
Aped from the crowd-face and the festive room,
And waiting lost and still
In the empty glass where it presents a will
That is not ours. Imagined, then, by whom?

I thought, our help is in all that is full-grown
In nature, and all that is with hands well-made,
Carved in verse or stone
Or a harvest yield. There is the harmony
By which we know our own and the world's health,
The simply good, great counterpoise
To blind nonentity,
Ever renewed and squandered wealth.
Yet not enough. Because we could not wait
To untwist the twisted smile and make it straight
Or render restitution to the tree.
We who were wrapped so warm in foolish joys
Did not have time to call on pity
For all that is sick, and heal and remake our city.

II

THE POET

And in bewilderment
My tongue shall tell
What mind had never meant
Nor memory stored.
In such bewilderment
Love's parable
Into the world was sent
To stammer its word.

What I shall never know
I must make known.
Where traveller never went
Is my domain.
Dear disembodiment
Through which is shown
The shapes that come and go
And turn again.

Heaven-sent perplexity—
If thought should thieve
One word of the mystery
All would be wrong.
Most faithful fantasy
That can believe
Its immortality
And make a song.

V

About the well of life where we are made
Spirits of earth and heaven together lie.
They do not turn their bright heads at our coming,
So deep their dream of pure commingled being,
So still the air and the level beam that flows
Along the ground, shed by the flowers and waters:
All above and beneath them a deep darkness.
Their bodies lie in shadow or buried in earth,
Their heads shine in the light of the underworld.
Loaded with fear and crowned with every hope
The born stream past them to the longed for place.

TO THE FORGOTTEN DEAD

Take the great road Oblivion
That does not cross the fields of fame
And princedoms burning bright in death.
You from time have gone away
For ever, and your eternity
Is too vast for story or name.
Once you stood and did not break
And were forgotten. Do not make
Your silent magnanimity
A mock at fame's importunate breath.

DIALOGUE

I never saw the world until that day,
The real fabulous world newly reborn,
And celebrated and crowned on every side
With sun and sky and lands of fruit and corn,
The dull ox and the high horse glorified,
Red images on the red clay,
And such a race of women and men,
I thought the famous ones had never died.
I speak in truth of what he showed me then.
But you whom he loved and yet could never dare
To win, how was it that you did not care
For such a man as he?
                            Oh he was dull,
Sick of the cheats of his phantasmal art
And that unending journey through no place,
He said, and asked to fly into the cool
And subterranean harbour of my heart,
Darker than his, more cool. He little thought

It was a riotous prison that he sought,
A place indeed, but such a place!
What could he give me, who was never his fool,
Nor Helen, nor Iseult, playing a harlot's part?
I have wondered what he read into my face.

I knew a man, the most unlike that one,
I think the shrewdest, sweetest man
I ever saw, modest and yet a king
Among his harvests, with a harvester's eye
That had forgotten to wonder why
At this or that, knowing his natural span,
And spoke of evil as "the other thing",
Judging a virtue as he judged the weather,
Endured, accepted all, the equal brother
Of men and chance, the good and the bad day.
And when I spoke of the high horse glorified,
He smiled and answered: Tell me, will it pull?
Or find its way in the dark? Is it on my side?
Then I'm its friend. But it must answer
To bit and rein. I do not want a dancer.
And yet he loved a good horse as a good
Workman or field or block of seasoned wood.
He was neither a plain nor a fanciful fool.
Yet that first world was beautiful
And true, stands still where first it stood.

I have known men and horses many a day.
Men come and go, the wise and the fanciful.
I ride my horse and make it go my way.

PETROL SHORTAGE

This mild late-winter afternoon
Everything's unfamiliar;
Vacant silence as of a peace
After a fifty-year-long war.

The planes are hunted from the sky,
All round me is the natural day.
I watch this empty country road
Roll half a century away.

And looking round me I recall
That here the patient ploughmen came
Long years ago, and so remember
What they were and what I am.

I think, the aeroplanes will pass,
Power's stupendous equipage,
And leave with simpler dynasties
The mute detritus of an age.

The daring pilot will come down,
Cold marble wings will mark his place,
And soft persuasion of the grass
Restrain the swiftest of his race.

The cycle will come round again,
Earth will repair its broken day,
And pastoral Europe dream again
Of little wars waged far away.

A week refutes a prophecy
That only ages can make true.
The deafening distractions wait,
Industrious fiends, for me and you.

BALLAD OF EVERYMAN

I

Stout Everyman set out to meet
   His brothers gathered from every land,
And make a peace for all the earth
   And link the nations hand to hand.

He came into a splendid hall
   And there he saw a motionless dove
Swung from the roof, but for the rest
   Found little sign of peace or love.

Two days he listened patiently,
   But on the third got up and swore:
"Nothing but slaves and masters here:
   Your dove's a liar and a whore.

"Disguised police on the high seats,
   In every corner pimps and spies.
Goodbye to you; I'd rather be
   With friends in Hell or Paradise".

The great room turned to watch him go,
   But oh the deadly silence then.
From that day brave Everyman
   Was never seen by friend again.

II

Night after night I dream a dream
   That I am flying through the air
On some contraption old and lame
   As Icarus' unlucky chair.

And first I see the empty fields—
    No sign of Everyman anywhere—
And then I see a playing field
    And two great sides in combat there.

And then they change into a beast
    With iron hoofs and scourging tail
That treads a bloody harvest down
    In readiness for the murdering flail.

And then a rash of staring eyes
    Covers the beast, back, sides and head,
And stare as if remembering
    Something that long ago was said.

And the beast is gone, and nothing's there
    But murderers standing in a ring,
And at the centre Everyman.
    I never saw so poor a thing.

Curses upon the traitorous men
    Who brought our good friend Everyman down,
And murder peace to bring their peace,
    And flatter and rob the ignorant clown.

NIGHTMARE OF PEACE

    Even in a dream how were we there
    Among the commissars of peace
    And that meek humming in the air
    From the assenting devotees?
    Police disguised on every chair
    Up on the platform. Peace was there

In hands where it would never stir.
Aloft a battle-plated dove
Throned over all in menacing love.

But why was our old friend Everyman
Among this false-faced company
When we knew that he was sought
Across the border a mile away
By men the living spit of these?
He smiled and whispered he was not bought,
Left us and said he'd soon be back;
An old acquaintance waited below.
The whole room turned to watch him go,
And the eyes said, You will not come back.
Two hours passed: he did not come back.

Then as in dreams a swelling fear
Begets the palpable image, we
Were suddenly climbing through the air
In some contraption old and lame
As Icarus' handiwork. We flew on
Searching for hapless Everyman.
Indifferent fields, nothing to see.
Then suddenly a crowd, a pack
Of players in some archaic game?
So we would make the riddle say
Yet could not take our eyes away
And knew we were there, had known the same
In many a nightmare. Then it came:
A slowly lengthening horrible tail
Thrust from the ambiguous monster's back,
The calmly lazily waving thing
That brushes flies on a summer day.
A beast trampling as oxen tread
The annual yield, the harvest play.

For a moment: then we saw the lies
Spring open, watched the rows of eyes
Break out upon the animal's back.
And all dissolved in a common ring.
At the centre, truly dead,
Lay Everyman. So both were true,
Animal and human, and we knew
These were God's creatures after all
Ashamed and broken by the fall
Into the dark.
             Then one stepped out
Who had been but now a hoof or horn
Or drop of sweat on the animal,
And waved and shouted: we must come down.
And the animal was reborn.
We had crossed the border, must come down,
And were again in the conference hall
With Peace the Tyrant's pitiless law,
While still within our minds we saw
The beast trampling, Everyman down.

III

"THERE'S NOTHING HERE"

There's nothing here I can take into my hands.
Oh, for the plough stilts and the horse's reins,
And the furrows running free behind me.
The clay still clings to me here, and the heavy smell
Of peat and dung and cattle, and the taste of the dram
In my mouth, the last of all.
These things are what I was made for. Send me back.
There is not even a shadow here. How can I live
Without substance and shadow? Am I here
Because I duly read the Bible on Sundays
And drowsed through the minister's sermon? I knew my duty.
But in the evening
I led the young lads to the orra lasses
Across the sound to the other islands. Summer!
How can I live without summer? And the harvest moon
And the stooks that looked like little yellow graves, so bonny
And sad and strange, while I walked through them
For a crack with Jock at the bothy: old-farrant stories
He had, I could tell you some queer stories. And then we
   would dander
Among the farms to visit the lasses, climb
Through many a window till morning. But that's no talk
For this place. And then I think of the evenings
After the long day's work . . .

Note. This poem is probably a soliloquy by Edwin Muir's cousin
Sutherland, awaking after death to find himself in heaven. Similar
exploits of Sutherland's are described in Muir's autobiography. *Orra*
means without regular employment, working here and there as
required; *old-farrant* means old-fashioned; and *dander* means to dawdle
or stroll.

DIALOGUE

I have heard you cry:
"Oh that the impression of mortality
Would ease its hold and set me free!"
Your workaday face lined with immortal cares
As if you feared that unawares
The indestructible flowers of Paradise
Might suddenly droop and wither
In a brief, thoughtless intermission of your eyes
And all your journey thither
End in consummate vacancy.
And you reply: "All else shall fade but they".
But I:
"In a long afternoon, long, long ago,
I Adam awoke in the one and only eve
Of my sunsetting and beginning
And the first unending of evening.
How can I mourn for what I chose to leave?"
And you: "Chose you to leave?"
And I: "Or how deny
The starting point of this my only road
Where other flowers and other pleasures gem and bud
And all my kindred go,
Or find a different face from this one face
Twisted with tears and laughter,
And the commandment: 'To be, to be'?
On which I read: all is before and after,
Then since you are here, off with you, go abroad".
And you: "Death also says: To be".
And I, impatiently:
"Good man, you are here, not there.
Here you are not at ease, but must prefer
What you were born for, this your place,
Where all moves towards infinity

At a snail's or a bullet's pace,
Plods, hurries, dawdles: finding, choosing its rhyme,
Science gathering gossip of what's so small
And great, no eye can see it.
You must make friends with all
Then wait awhile; how can all things be done in time?
And you are in time".
And you: "I am a footstep from eternity
And cannot lift my foot".
And I:
"You have denied the root
And think there is nothing here but night and day,
Sun and moon, man and star,
And death will take away them all.
But I say
That these great nothings, man and sun and star,
Will say through nothingness: we are, we are".
And you: "I know too well the dupes of time.
Have you not heard them say:
'Do be in time, be sure you are in time',
With such a strange anxiety?
And once or twice these words: 'Oh, let me be,
Do let me be'.
As if drab Penury itself were trying to say
Through these poor lips . . .

"THE HEART COULD NEVER SPEAK"

The heart could never speak
But that the Word was spoken.
We hear the heart break
Here with hearts unbroken.
Time, teach us the art
That breaks and heals the heart.

Heart, you would be dumb
But that your word was said
In time, and the echoes come
Thronging from the dead.
Time, teach us the art
That resurrects the heart.

Tongue, you can only say
Syllables, joy and pain,
Till time, having its way,
Makes the word live again.
Time, merciful lord,
Grant us to learn your word.

"I SEE THE IMAGE"

I see the image of a naked man,
He stoops and picks a smooth stone from the ground,
Turns round and in a wide arc flings it backward
Towards the beginning. What will catch it,
Hand, or paw, or gullet of sea-monster?
He stoops again, turns round and flings a stone
Straight on before him. I listen for its fall,
And hear a ringing on some hidden place
As if against the wall of an iron tower.

"OUR APPREHENSIONS GIVE"

Our apprehensions give
Us to another time, and cast
Our hapless horoscope; we did not live
Either in the present or the past.

And thus afloat upon our fears
We scarcely lived, and dread to be.
Straight on the reckless pilot sheers;
Our sons are born upon the sea,

And in the waves will live and die,
Not drift to the murderous strand
But reading for portents in the sky,
Knowing too well, too well, the land.

"THE REFUGEES BORN FOR A LAND UNKNOWN"

The refugees born for a land unknown
We have dismissed their wrongs, now dull and old,
And little judgment days lost in the dark.

"I have fled through land and sea, blank land and sea,
Because my house is besieged by murderers
And I was wrecked in the ocean, crushed and swept,
Spilling salt angry tears on the salt waves,
My life waste water drawn down through a hole,
Yet lived. And now with alien eyes I see
The flowering trees on the unreal hills,
And in an English garden all afternoon
I watch the bees among the lavender.
Bees are at home, and think they have their place,
And I outside.
Footsteps on the stairs, two heavy, two light,
The door opens. Since then I remember nothing,
But this room in a place where no doors open.
I think the world died many years ago".

"AND ONCE I KNEW"

And once I knew
A hasty man,
So small, so kind, and so perfunctory,
Of such an eager kindness
It flushed his little face with standing shame.

Wherever he came
He poured his alms into a single hand
That was full then empty. He could not understand.
A foolish or a blessed blindness,
Saint or fool, a better man than you.

SUNSET

Fold upon fold of light,
Half-heaven of tender fire,
Conflagration of peace,
Wide hearth of the evening world.
How can a cloud give peace,
Peace speak through bodiless fire
And still the angry world?

Yet now each bush and tree
Stands still within the fire,
And the bird sits on the tree.
Three horses in a field
That yesterday ran wild
Are bridled and reined by light
As in a heavenly field.
Man, beast and tree in fire,
The bright cloud showering peace.

THE DAY BEFORE THE LAST DAY

If it could come to pass, and all kill all
And in a day or a week we could destroy
Ourselves, that is the beginning only
Of the destruction, for so we murder all
That ever has been, all species and forms,
Man and woman and child, beast and bird,
Tree, flower and herb, and that by which they were known,
Sight and hearing and touch, feeling and thought,
And memory of our friends among the dead.
If there were only a single ear that listening heard
A footstep coming nearer, it would bring
Annunciation of the world's resurrection.
A sound! We would not know even the silence
Where all was now as if it had never been.

Mechanical parody of the Judgment Day
That does not judge but only deals damnation.
Let us essay a hypothetical picture.

"All these and all alone in death's last day.
Before them stretches the indifferent ocean
Where no wave lifts its head and stagnant water
Lies spent against the shore. Yet as they wait
A wan light from the east falls on their faces
And they cannot bear the light, and hide in the ground,
Yet have no comfort there, for all are alone.
And there awaken the dark ancestral dreams.
They dream that the grave and the sea give up their dead
In wonder at the news of the death of death,
Hearing that death itself is balked by death.
And those who were drowned a year or a thousand years
Come out with staring eyes, foam on their faces,
And quaint sea-creatures fixed like jewelled worms

Upon their salt-white crowns, sea-tangle breasts,
That they, the once dead, might know the second death.
And then a stir and rumour break their dream,
As men and women at the point of death
Rise from their beds and clasp the ground in hope
Imploring sanctuary from grass and root
That never failed them yet and seemed immortal.
And women faint with child-birth lay their babes
Beside them on the earth and turn away
And lovers two by two estranged for ever
Lie each in place without a parting look.
And the dying awakened know
That the generous do not try to help their neighbours,
Nor the feeble and greedy ask for succour,
Nor the fastidious complain of their company
Nor the ambitious dream of a great chance lost
Nor the preacher try to save one soul. For all
Think only of themselves and curse the faithless earth.
The sun rises above the sea, and they look and think:
'We shall not watch its setting'. And all get up
And stare at the sun. But they hear no great voice crying:
'There shall be no more time, nor death, nor change,
Nor fear, nor hope, nor longing, nor offence,
Nor need, nor shame'. But all are silent, thinking:
'Choose! Choose again, you who have chosen this!
Too late! Too late!'
And then: 'Where and by whom shall we be remembered?'"

Imaginary picture of a stationary fear.

"I HAVE BEEN TAUGHT"

I have been taught by dreams and fantasies
Learned from the friendly and the darker phantoms
And got great knowledge and courtesy from the dead
Kinsmen and kinswomen, ancestors and friends
But from two mainly
Who gave me birth.

Have learned and drunk from that unspending good
These founts whose learned windings keep
My feet from straying
To the deadly path

That leads into the sultry labyrinth
Where all is bright and the flare
Consumes and shrivels
The moist fruit.

Have drawn at last from time which takes away
And taking leaves all things in their right place
An image of forever
One and whole.

And now that time grows shorter, I perceive
That Plato's is the truest poetry,
And that these shadows
Are cast by the true.

INDEX OF FIRST LINES